DEVELOPING
PHONICS
SKILLS

LISTENING, SPEAKING, READING, AND WRITING

Consultants

Lucile T. Robinson, Ph.D., General Consultant,
Ontario-Montclair School District,
Ontario, California

Olive M. Amundson, B. A., Reading Specialist,
El Rancho Unified School District,
Pico Rivera, California

DEVELOPING PHONICS SKILLS

LISTENING, SPEAKING, READING, AND WRITING

LOUISE BINDER SCOTT
Ed.M.

Teachers College, Columbia University
New York and London   1982

Published by Teachers College Press, 1234 Amsterdam Avenue,
New York, N.Y. 10027

Library of Congress Cataloging in Publication Data

Scott, Louise Binder.
  Developing phonics skills.

  Includes index.
  1. Reading (Elementary)—Phonetic method. I. Title.
LB1573.3.S37   372.4′145   81-23225
                      AACR2

ISBN 0-8077-2718-0

All poems, stories, and other creative activities are the
original work of Louise Binder Scott unless otherwise specified.

Handwriting models in this book are reproduced with permission of
Zaner-Bloser, Inc., from the series *Creative Growth with Handwriting*,
© 1975, 1979.

Manufactured in the United States of America

87 86 85 84 83 82   1 2 3 4 5 6

CONTENTS

IV

PHONICS IN SPEAKING ACTIVITIES 50

V

PHONICS IN READING ACTIVITIES 97

VI

PHONICS IN WRITING ACTIVITIES 149

VII

LEARNING AND IMPROVING THE SOUNDS OF ENGLISH   175

INTRODUCTION

*D*eveloping *Phonics Skills* is a non-technical guide to teaching phonics through the four communication skills: listening, speaking, reading, and writing. This book is designed for primary classroom teachers, parents, teachers of children needing remedial reading help in middle grades, curriculum consultants who wish to give phonics a more thorough treatment through workshops, remedial reading specialists, and teachers of children who speak English as a second language or use substandard speech. Phonics should be taught daily as part of the reading program.

To learn to read, one first must learn to listen and speak, for words become meaningful only when they have been used orally and comprehension has been established. To learn to write, one first must learn to listen, to speak, and to read, for the symbols used in writing become significant only as they have been heard and encountered in printed form in a variety of ways. The organization of this book follows the traditional pattern for development of the communication skills, with consecutive chapters discussing the phonics principles and suggesting ways of using phonics in listening, speaking, reading, and writing activities.

It is virtually impossible to separate one communication skill from another in teaching, for each is highly dependent upon one or more of the others for usage and meaning. These skills have been interrelated throughout the book, none standing as a separate entity, but overlapping the others. A child is taught through games, devices, and activities to listen for beginning consonants while becoming aware of the speech mechanism that produces those sounds. The child recognizes both upper- and lower-case letter forms and makes the strokes necessary for writing them. Briefly, the child must recall letter sound, letter name, and letter form in one three-way relationship.

The activities contained in *Developing Phonics Skills* have been designated as to kindergarten, first-, second-, third-, or fourth-grade level. Most of the content is applicable to several levels, however. The teacher or parent is advised to adapt the materials to specific needs of the children being taught. The instructor should remember that some second graders can perform as well as or even better than some third or fourth graders and that some third and fourth graders are functioning at first- or second-grade levels. Teachers of children who are learning English as a second language will find this book useful for moving children quickly into pronouncing and learning the sounds of English.

It is recommended that the instructor modify activities to include words from readers with which the children are familiar so that phonics skills will relate to daily work.

Developing Phonics Skills contains techniques and ideas for preparing reading charts, spelling lessons, visual aids, and duplications and many language arts activities related to such special occasions as holidays. This plan will enable a teacher to incorporate phonics into subject areas each day.

The book's organization will enable the instructor to locate ideas with ease. Materials for developing key words, consonant sounds, consonant blends, consonant digraphs, short vowels, long vowels, other vowels, and special endings are presented in that order when these topics are relevant to a particular chapter.

Although the chapters follow a basic sequential plan for teaching essential elements of a phonics program, each chapter has been arranged to meet specific needs of a particular skill and may be used with any reading program.

Chapter I describes the process of learning to read through the use of sensory stimuli. It emphasizes readiness for phonics and discusses the two approaches: synthetic and analytic. It especially emphasizes readiness, preliminary phonics experiences, and the need for teaching phonics skills. Phonics concepts that will be amplified in subsequent chapters are introduced.

Chapter II provides ideas for parents' use at home or at school.

Chapter III is concerned with auditory learning, since speaking, reading, and writing skills depend upon how well a child can attend to, assimilate, and recall what is heard.

Chapter IV emphasizes the speech sounds of the English language. No child masters one sound at a time when learning to speak. A teacher works from the whole word, phrase, or sentence. When a child understands ideas and meanings, he or she refines words and speech sounds within that context. One would not ask a child to hear the sounds in *cat* if the child were not familiar with the meaning of the word and the animal itself. So it is with learning to speak, read, and write. The whole provides meaning, and only after a child comprehends meaning can we begin the process of analysis, breaking down the unit into parts. On the other hand, if one speech sound is garbled and indistinct, it may be necessary to isolate it so that the child can hear accurately what is happening when the sound is misarticulated. The same process applies to a written or printed word, which cannot be pronounced or recalled unless it is dissected, heard, and the error corrected.

Lesson plans and exercises for applying consonant sounds to words are included in the sequence in which a child learns to articulate sounds, from the easiest to the most difficult. Chapters III and IV concern listening and speech and are powerfully linked, helping to transfer talk to the printed and written word, which represents a special way of talking.

Chapter V deals with the degrees to which children come to an understanding of the purposes and processes of applying speech sounds to reading. Since phonics cannot be separated from reading, the teacher will understand how to apply those skills of auditory identification and discrimination of speech-sound production to the reading process. This chapter provides stories, games, and various ideas for teaching all the elements of phonics: consonants, consonant digraphs, consonant clusters or blends, and vowels.

Chapter VI stresses prewriting and tactile-kinesthetic activities. Since letter name, sound, and form must become one association, the shape of alphabet letters and whole words are emphasized. To see a whole word with accuracy, a child must necessarily see its parts as distinguished from one another. Stories, mnemonic devices, rhymes, and other activities are provided for writing practice.

Chapter VII emphasizes how children who use English as a second language or substandard speech can be helped.

Appendix I offers definitions of terms used throughout the book. These terms concern the four communication skills, their aspects, and the reading process itself.

Appendix II lists a bank of roots, or phonograms, on which words that rhyme can be built.

Appendix III presents phonics rules or generalizations.

Educators agree that phonics is a method of teaching *word analysis*, not a method of teaching reading. If the latter were so, we would have a nation of "word sounders." There is no single method of teaching reading, but there is a single goal. A child must be able to read orally and silently with confidence, assurance, fluency, understanding, and interest. The goal is achieved in different ways. Yet, as a technique for training in independent word attack, the phonics approach in helping children to acquire this ability has never been replaced by an adequate substitute. Phonics calls for observation, comparison, and analysis. It compels a child to think through possibilities, try out rules, make appropriate generalizations, and reach conclusions.

These days the question asked is "What phonics method is most effective?" not "Should we teach phonics?" Today's studies show that children given early alphabet and phonics training seem to have a greater confidence and ability to decode words, whereas the child taught solely by a "look-say" method or by phonics taught in a hit-or-miss fashion becomes confused when asked to attack an unknown word. The nature of phonics advocated here—phonics that incorporates all sensory avenues of learning in natural sequence and gives proper representation to all communication skills, listening, speaking, reading, and writing—concerns a total process of language development and is not concerned with unrelated, isolated symbols.

AN ANALOGY

A child goes to the cloakroom. There are 30 coats hanging on racks. The child's coat may be blue, and there may be no need to look for another coat. Or there may be five other blue coats, so additional clues to identity may be needed: the sleeves, the black buttons, the plaid lining, the fur collar, or the fuzzy material. The child may require only one clue or several. By the same token, some children will require only one initial consonant or vowel letter to recognize a word. Others may learn through the word's shape, the way the word ends, the position and configuration of certain letters, the way the word appeals to the sense of taste or smell, if the word rhymes, or they recall a generalization that applies. Another child may "try on" a word several times to see if it makes sense in a phrase or sentence. In every case, however, children must recognize the word as one they have heard spoken.

I

DEVELOPING PHONICS SKILLS

Learning to read begins at birth. From that moment, children are preparing themselves, under the guidance of people in their environment, primarily the family, for the time when they will be ready to look at a page of printed symbols and derive meaning from it. Progress can be noted in many ways as children grow, for they learn to read in sensory areas long before they understand words on the printed page.

Children learn to read with their eyes. Visual discrimination begins early with recognitions of people in the family and neighborhood and the ability to distinguish personal belongings. This visual skill is expanded as children note likenesses and differences in objects around them.

Children learn to read with their fingers. Daddy's moustache, a sticky lollipop, an icy wind, and shapes of objects provide early tactile experiences. These experiences will be used later to help the child with writing skills.

Children learn to read with the sense of smell. Olfactory stimuli, such as a freshly baked cake, the fragrance of flowers, and the odor of clean sheets, become meaningful, form mental images, and are eventually applicable to formal reading.

Children learn to read with the sense of taste. Gustatory sensations bring to mind buttered popcorn, lemonade, and apples. Behavior patterns arising out of the sense of taste are established very early in every young life.

The development of these skills in sensory discrimination is an essential element in the reading readiness program.

PHONETICS AND PHONICS

What Is Phonetics? Phonetics is the study of the speech sounds, or phonemes, of a language. Whether we deal with speaking or reading, we find ourselves confronted with the formulation, transmission, and reception of language symbols that are the sounds of speech.

What Is Phonics? Phonics is the application of the speech sounds to reading, writing, and spelling. The child is required to use a system of trial and error combined with controlled association. The similarities between problem solving and phonics are plentiful. Young learners do not use random behavior. They must explore possibilities and apply rules or generalizations that may or may not work.

PHONICS CONCEPTS
IN THIS BOOK

Following are the elements of phonics that have been considered in presenting suggestions for teaching the concepts in listening, speaking, reading, and writing activities, in that order.

○   *Key words.* A key word is one that has been selected as a sample. Usually it is a noun accompanied by a picture, and it helps the child recall other words beginning with the same initial letter sound or word segment.

○   *Single consonants.* Children will learn to recognize single consonants aurally and visually in initial, medial, and final word positions. They will discover that there are more sounds than letters since some letters contain more than one sound.

2

○ *Consonant digraphs.* Children will note that certain consonants appear together as two-letter combinations but produce only one sound.
○ *Consonant blends.* Children will observe that two or three consonants side by side will produce clusters or blends, as *fl* in *flag* and *str* in *street.*
○ *Vowels.* Children will realize that each word must have a vowel and that a vowel can have several different sounds.
○ *Vowel combinations.* Children will see that vowels can be used in combinations to produce new sounds, as *oo* in *moon* and in *book,* or vowel blends or digraphs, as *oy* in *boy* and *ou* in *house.*
○ *Special endings.* Children will learn that basic root words can be modified to create new words or tenses by the addition of such endings as *ed, es,* or *ing.*

DESIGNATION BY GRADE LEVEL

The greatest challenge facing a teacher is the improvement of classroom practices. Instructors need a wealth of ideas and resources to implement the communication skills program in progress and help forestall reading problems.

Because prevention of problems will hasten learning, many suggestions are geared to early primary grades. Grade levels are suggested as guides and are not intended to be restrictive. Most teachers are flexible and are willing to experiment with all activities as individual and group needs arise.

DO ALL CHILDREN NEED PHONICS?

Some children read almost intuitively, apparently skipping intermediate steps and figuring out their own methods of analyzing words. If we were to subject them to a step-by-step sounding process, we would do nothing except entangle their thinking like that of the centipede when asked which leg comes after which. The author advises that children attempt to make their own discoveries in reading as they do in mathematics. Over-helping children sometimes can slow the pace and cause them to feel inadequate, depriving them of the joy of using their own pickaxes to mine gold. Slow readers and those children learning English as a second language need sound, word, and phrase drill because the subconscious mind does not yet have its own method of connecting symbol with sound or word. Those children must be given logical assistance to help them work out new words.

3

There is no assurance that any group of methods will work effectively for all children, and, therefore, a constellation of ideas must be pursued. Success in using the contents of this book will depend upon how well the teacher or parent can translate concepts into action.

APPROACHES TO TEACHING PHONICS AND READING

Reading is a highly skilled activity, involving an integration of many mental processes. Letter and word shapes are combined in different ways. Each shape has a meaning. Alphabet letters are associated with particular sounds, and one letter can have more than one sound.

Methods for teaching phonics sometimes are divided into two systems: analytic and synthetic. Most teachers use an eclectic method in order to accommodate all individuals. Approaches explained here are both employed in most instances. The more varied the approaches used, the greater the degree of learning that will likely take place.

Analytic Approach. Emphasis is placed upon the shapes of words by pictorial representation. Service words, such as *they*, *saw*, and *was*, are needed to form complete sentences. Service words usually are spelled irregularly and cannot be decoded easily by children. Work on parts in relation to the whole is provided. Discovery and the process of writing are significant.

Phonics analysis is included and involves the ability to identify sounds of the English language, the symbols devised to represent them, and the association of sound with symbol.

Synthetic Approach. Children learn the names of the letters, their shapes, and their sequences. Left-to-right orientation and word-attack drill are provided. Pupils learn that one letter can stand for different sounds. They pronounce sounds in word context, using a system of blending the sounds to produce words. Auditory discrimination is important, as well as letter configuration and writing as a means of strengthening other skills.

TEACHING GENERALIZATIONS

Whether to use an analytic or a synthetic approach to teaching reading is beside the point. Sooner or later, some children will formulate rules for themselves. Many children will not, however.

Generalizations concern a consistent relationship of letters and sounds and their positions within words. Generalizations or rules (stated in appendix III) will provide inexperienced readers with clues for translating written or printed symbols to sounds. Teachers should use discretion as to whether or when a generalization should be taught.

It is unfortunate but probably unavoidable that there is no agreement on guidelines for teaching phonics. Disagreements concern

o   How many concepts children require to master a decoding system
o   How individual children differ in their abilities to acquire phonics skills
o   What phonics teaching is needed at each grade level to ensure that a child will have the confidence to work out words

Serious consideration should be given to teaching separately the concepts of consonants, vowels, digraphs, blends, and so on.

One can find lists of exceptions that do not conform to specific generalizations. Dictionaries contain many unusually spelled words, as do compiled basal-word lists; yet, many of those basal words can be rhymed with other words, using intrinsically the same spelling as that of words having partially familiar segments that lend themselves to comparison.

Don McCabe, in using 220 Dolch sight words, discovered that 170 of them were "sufficiently patterned to teach via the word family approach."[1] He took a segment from a Dolch word and asked pupils to build other words from it; thus, the sight word *black* became *back*, *sack*, and so on. He divided the list into easier half and harder half and discovered diagnostically which words a child needed to learn by sight. He called these 54 words "loners" because they did not have families. Many of these words, although having no families, still had some familiar parts; yet they required separate teaching.

Using the criterion that generalizations or phonics rules must have 100 percent applicability should not be considered. If the rules are useful 50 percent of the time, deductions can still be made by some children. The fact that generalizations may not always work is no reason to dispense with them altogether. Trial-and-error experiences will merely add to a child's cognitive development and instill an investigative attitude toward reading. This is not to condemn a whole-word method of teaching reading. Whole or sight words, such as *the*, *who*, and *one*, are needed to build contextual vocabulary through phrases and sentences that give children immediate experiences with reading.

---

[1]Don McCabe, "220 Sight Words Are Too Many for Students with Memories Like Mine," *The Reading Teacher*, April 1978, pp. 791–93.

READINESS FOR PHONICS

Most of the general readiness factors also apply to readiness for phonics.

- Do children show curiosity about words?
- Do they ask a parent or teacher for identification of a word?
- Are they interested in books?
- Can they listen to a story being read?
- Do they express a desire to read?
- Can they follow simple directions?
- Can they distinguish similarities and differences among the sounds around them?
- Can they discriminate one speech sound from another? *Bat* from *cat?*
- Can they recognize words that rhyme?
- Can they remember and reproduce a series of abstract shapes in the right order?
- Can they note differences in shapes, pictures, and objects?
- Can they recognize circles, squares, rectangles, and triangles? Manuscript letters are composed of circles, half circles, straight lines, slant lines, and curves.
- Can they match groups of letters?
- Is their muscular coordination adequate?
- Can they spell their own names?
- Do they know their home addresses and telephone numbers?

These are only a few preparatory steps. Years of research and study have never revealed a magic clue that will indicate the state of readiness other than that which is revealed by children themselves.

It is important that readiness for the reading process be considered before phonics concepts are presented. Here are preliminary phonics experiences the teacher may provide.

PRELIMINARY PHONICS EXPERIENCES

- Emphasize left-to-right movements by placing objects in that order or arranging pictures on the flannel board or along the chalk rail.
- Transcribe and read children's verbalizations and experiences.
- Arrange stories and pictures and ask children to retell the events in sequence.
- Suggest memorizing and dramatizing nursery rhymes and easy-to-learn poems.

○ Employ many listening activities.
○ Use finger plays, records, and alphabet songs.
○ Display the upper- and lower-case alphabet in sequence.
○ Make picture dictionaries.
○ Give practice in producing speech sounds.
○ Provide learning centers where children can browse through books.
○ Give children tracing experiences around templates, in finger paint, and on paper. Supply blunt scissors for cutting. Encourage scribbling activities.
○ Label objects in the room.
○ Offer visual experiences that include differentiating colors and shapes, seriating objects from large to small (and vice versa), and designating objects on the basis of their positions around the room.

Parents can supervise many of these activities.

LEARNING PHONICS AND READING TERMINOLOGY

Studies have been conducted concerning children's need to learn the terminology of phonics and reading: consonant, consonant digraph, consonant blend, and so on. Some educators object to children's learning these terms. It is taken for granted that kindergartners and first graders would not benefit from such designations. Yet, most second graders have heard the teacher use these words so frequently that they have become a part of their vocabularies.

If the terminology is part of the teacher's vocabulary, children will gradually absorb it. Certainly by third or fourth grade they can handle the terms *schwa* and *diphthong* for by that time they are using dictionaries in which those terms are described. As one second-grade teacher remarked: "I tell it like it is. If it is a diphthong, I call it a diphthong. I use the proper descriptive language as soon as the children encounter the phonic or reading concept." If phonics is taught sequentially, the correct terminology will be absorbed and fall into place.

TEACHING LETTER NAMES

Long before entering kindergarten, children are exposed to alphabet letter names through ABC songs, "Sesame Street" programs, and the spelling of their names. Educational toys are geared to alphabet learning. A child with a retentive mind will find it easy to absorb rhythmic ABCs and repeat them rote fashion. This is mere jargon, however, until letters can be applied to reading and writing, where association and context will give them meaning.

TEACHING LETTER FORMS

Letters of the alphabet are the symbols children must learn to recognize in varying combinations and printed words if they are to acquire the skill of reading. As noted previously, children must establish a relationship of the letter name, sound, and form or configuration. This can be accomplished by providing experiences and activities that incorporate all three concepts. Consequently, writing or using letter forms becomes an integral part of learning letter names. Yet, most children will need to write a letter form many times before they can recall relationships. Like any other skill, writing requires sensory training as a foundation. Before a child begins to write on paper, he or she should experience many prewriting activities: tracing lines, circles, and other shapes in the air, in wet sand, and on paper with finger paint or with crayon.

The shapes activities include the elements needed later for formal writing and are dealt with in chapter VI.

TEACHING LETTER SOUNDS

Some teachers begin training in phonics as soon as a child has learned two or three sight words beginning with the same letter sound, for example, *see, said, some.* Other teachers delay the teaching until a child has acquired an appreciable sight vocabulary. All basal series include letter sounds taught at intervals for recognition of vowels, initial consonants, blends, digraphs, and so on.

The author advocates beginning auditory discrimination of consonant speech sounds in kindergarten. This phase of the phonics program should emphasize identification of initial speech sounds in children's names and in names of pictures and vocal production of the speech sound within the word. Key words should be chosen for this purpose. Sounds may be isolated whenever feasible, as "ssss" or "rrrr" in *see* or *run.* These sounds may be given characteristics or personalities, as the "snake" or "rooster" sound.

Consonants are more constant than vowels in the way they are pronounced, but at the same time are misarticulated more frequently than vowels, except by bilingual groups. Problems may arise because of certain language characteristics. There are about 44 consonant and vowel sounds in the English language and only 26 alphabet letters to represent them. Two of these letters have blended sounds—*x* and *q.* Two have more

Table 1.   KEY WORDS

a:	*apple* or *ant* (short *a*)	o:	*ox* or *octopus* (short *o*)
b:	*bed* or *bell* (short *e*)	p:	*pan* or *pig* (short *a* or *i*)
c:	*cat* or *cap* (short *a*)	q:	*queen* or *quilt* (long *e* or short *i*)
d:	*duck* or *doll* (short *u*, short *o*)	r:	*rat* or *rug* (short *a* or *u*)
e:	*elf* or *egg* (short *e*)	s:	*sun* or *sock* (short *u* or *o*)
f:	*fish* or *fan* (short *i* or *a*)	t:	*top* or *tub* (short *o* or *u*)
g:	*gum* or *gate* (short *u*, long *a*)	u:	*umbrella* (short *u*)
h:	*hat* or *hen* (short *a* or *e*)		(Note: There are few nouns
i:	*igloo* or *ink* (short *i*)		beginning with short *u*.)
j:	*jug* or *jam* (short *u* or *a*)	v:	*van* or *vine* (short *a* or long *i*)
k:	*kit* or *kite* (short or long *i*)	w:	*wig* (short *i*)
l:	*lamp* or *leaf* (short *a* or long *e*)	x:	*box* or *six* (short *or* or *i*)
m:	*mop* or *man* (short *o* or *a*)	y:	*yo-yo* (long *o*)
n:	*nut* or *net* (short *u* or *e*)	z:	*zebra* (long *e*)

than one pronunciation, *g* and *c*. Each of the vowels has at least more than one pronunciation.

KEY WORDS

Usually, one begins phonics instruction with a list of key or reference words, such as the list in table 1. The child recalls a key word because it begins with a certain consonant or vowel (usually a short vowel) and is monosyllabic, except in instances where such words are unavailable. If familiar short-vowel words cannot be located, long-vowel words may be used. Suggest that children compile a list of their own key words.

VOICED AND VOICELESS SPEECH SOUNDS

Often there is confusion over differences between voiced and voiceless speech sounds. For example, it is possible for consonant digraph *th* to be voiced (*they*) and also to be voiceless (*thumb*). Another example is the "s" sound. The vocal cords do not vibrate when saying "sss." On the other hand, *s* takes the sound of *z* in *dogs* and in *beds*.

Some educators may feel that emphasizing voiced and voiceless speech sounds is unimportant, and this is not debated. In order to teach phonics, a teacher should possess far more knowledge than might be offered to

Table 2. PAIRED VOICELESS AND VOICED CONSONANT SOUNDS

VOICELESS		VOICED	
p:	pan	b:	bed
t:	top	d:	duck
f:	fan	v:	van
k:	kite	g:	gum
s:	sun	z:	zebra
h:	hat		—
ch:	chick	j:	jam
sh:	shell	zh:	television
wh:	wheel	w:	wig
th:	thumb	th:	they
	—	l	
	—	m	
	—	n	
	—	ng	
	—	r	
	—	y	

q is a combination of *k* and *w* as in *queen* ("kween").
x is a combination of *k* and *s* as in *box* ("boks").

children. Each teacher should be guided by the classroom situation as to the amount of information needed to present a concept.

PAIRED CONSONANTS

Most of the letter sounds in our language are paired, or cognate, sounds; that is, the two consonant sounds are produced almost alike with the speech mechanism except that one is voiced (has vocal cord vibration) and the other is voiceless (has no vocal cord vibration). Paired consonant and consonant digraph words are listed in table 2.

CONSONANT DIGRAPHS

Unfortunately, consonant digraphs and consonant blends are sometimes confused. A consonant digraph contains two alphabet letters which produce one sound. Examples are: *sh*, *ch*, *ng*, *th* (voiced and voiceless), *ph*, *gh*, *wh*, and *zh*.

CONSONANT BLENDS
OR CLUSTERS

A consonant blend consists of two or three consonants in consecutive order such as *st* or *str*. Some authorities believe that, once a child has learned the names and sounds of the alphabet letters, the blends need not be presented. Yet, some children who have learned only an initial letter for word recognition may form a fixation upon that one letter and use it as a sole word-recognition clue. The blend concept should not be ignored and should be included in the continuum. A child who may be omitting the *s* sound in *stop* should be aware that there are two sounds to be blended. Blends are usually presented as units—*sm, tw, pr,* and so on—so accurate comparison between words beginning with consonant blends can be made. The main purpose of teaching the blend is to avoid pauses or junctures between the pronunciation of letters, as in *t-r-ee* = *tree*.

Most publishers, in their reading manuals, include initial and final consonant blends, three-letter clusters (*spr*), and combinations of blend and digraph (*thread* and *bench*). One major publisher uses blends exhaustively in its second- and third-grade readers.

Inform children that *sm, tr,* and *pl* do not make two separate sounds or only one letter sound. The two letter sounds blend together with no breath or pause in between, yet each sound maintains its own identity. Table 3 is a chart of the consonant blends.

Table 3.   THE CONSONANT BLENDS

THE s BLENDS

sc:	*scarf*	sk:	*skate*	sm:	*smoke*
sl:	*sled*	sn:	*snake*	sp:	*spoon*
squ:	*square*	st:	*star*	sw:	*swing*

THREE-LETTER CONSONANT BLENDS

str:	*street*	spr:	*spring*	scr:	*screen*

THE l BLENDS

bl:	*block*	gl:	*globe*	cl:	*clock*
fl:	*flock*	pl:	*plate*	sl:	*sled*

(continued)

11

Table 3 (*Continued*)

THE r BLENDS

br:	*broom*	fr:	*frog*	gr:	*grapes*
cr:	*crew*	dr:	*drum*	tr:	*tree*

OTHER BLENDS

tw:	*twins*	dw:	*dwarf*	shr:	*shrink*

BLENDING THE CONSONANT AND VOWEL

Blending is the essence of phonics. We do not articulate isolated sounds when we speak. Movements that produce individual phonemes must be made so rapidly that it is impossible to hear certain sounds within the context of a word. The components of *c-a-t* progress from left to right and formulate the whole word *cat*, but sharp hearing is needed to be able to discern three phonemes, unless the short *a* vowel is prolonged. Blending is the process of operating a decoding system smoothly and slowly so that there will be no audible break between sounds, as in *f-i-sh*; however, one can prolong each sound as *fff-i-shhhh* so a child can hear three sounds.

Before children can blend sounds, they must have some knowledge of phoneme (sound)–grapheme (written symbol) relationships. This ability necessitates synthesizing the sounds and relating separate elements into a whole word. How does the letter sound appear? How does it sound? How does it feel inside the mouth and on the lips?

As soon as children are able to make the association of letter name, sound, and form and treat the three concepts as one association, they are ready for that first step in blending and pronouncing the initial consonant and its succeeding vowel as a unit (consonant–short vowel blend, as in *ca* and *pi*). Short-vowel words are usually taught first in the blending practice because they are relatively easy for children to visualize, hear, and differentiate.

The teacher may ask pupils to pronounce the initial consonant and short vowel, such as *ra*, *fa*, *sa*, and then immediately add the final consonant, as in *ra-t*, *fa-n*, and *sa-t*. One concept of blending can show one sound gliding into another:

12

$$f \rightarrow a \qquad fa \rightarrow n \qquad fan$$

It is necessary that children be taught the art of blending through listening and speech. They will then arrive more easily and quickly at the correct pronunciation of the written or printed word.

TEACHING SPEECH SOUNDS
IN ISOLATION

The sounds of speech have another characteristic that is used in teaching phonics. Certain letter sounds, including all the vowel sounds, can be prolonged as long as the breath stream holds out, with pure quality of the sound still maintained. Other sounds must be terminated with an abrupt explosive effect, for the effort to prolong them will result in the production of vowel sounds, such as "buh" for *b* or "duh" for *d*.

Another confusing practice is for the teacher to distort sounds of initial consonants. *Bat* may be pronounced as "buh-at" and *let* as "ul-et." These distortions, of course, do not represent sounds heard in normal, connected speech. To avoid this problem of creating auditory confusions in the minds of children, the instructor is advised to teach the consonant–short vowel blend, as in *ba-t* and *ru-n*.

Synthesis of speech sounds is discussed and used more thoroughly in chapter IV.

II

PARENTS AS HELPERS

Many teachers recognize the importance of eliciting parents' cooperation, realizing that their assistance is invaluable and will partly solve the problem of providing individual help in overlarge classes. Teachers may define certain areas where parental help in the classroom is appreciated, or they may welcome ideas suggested by the parents themselves.

Knowledge, experience, and skill are required for teaching children to read. Yet, parents can contribute both at home and at school in many ways. Most parents appreciate specific suggestions from the teacher, for they want their help to be effective. They can guide children in improving their reading skills by listening to the child read, by helping him or her to work out new words, and by making simple devices or visual aids that will develop concepts associated with the printed word in its many forms. Once parents understand how speech sounds are produced and combined to form words, they can help children to interpret symbols and see and hear word patterns. Choosing from the many activities in this book and discovering at what age a child can participate in a particular activity is an important first parental step.

Nicholas P. Criscuolo describes ways in which parents can keep informed of their child's reading progress.[1] They may be invited to the school to observe the reading programs in action and to serve as paid tutors or paraprofessionals. Instructors can explain the reading program in ways that are understandable and meaningful. The New Haven, Connecticut, local newspaper offers a column for parents. It does not "talk down," but answers parents' questions regarding reading problems. One school in another city provides a Resource Room where parents meet informally and discuss the reading programs. Parents make scrapbooks, puppets, and other visual aids to take home or use at school. They also borrow reading and phonics materials.

Elsewhere, a committee of reading teachers develops homework assignments in English and Spanish for parents to take home. Cassidy and Vukelich state, "Research has shown that parents can, with the proper training, function as their children's teachers."[2]

In some programs, parents received direct instruction in teaching their children reading skills and cooperated with the teachers by giving supplementary instruction at home. Workshops were held, and games were played and constructed. Researchers reported that parents can effectively enhance their children's prereading and reading skills. These authors felt that parental involvement was particularly relevant and valuable.

The devices and activities contained in this book are easy for a teacher or a lay person to follow and suggest ways in which parents can assist their children not only at school but also at home.

WAYS PARENTS CAN ASSIST THEIR CHILDREN AT HOME

Parents can help their children at home in many ways by

○ Reading to their children regularly
○ Having high educational aspirations for their children and showing interest in their progress

[1]Nicholas P. Criscuolo, "Activities That Help to Involve Parents in Reading," *The Reading Teacher*, vol. 32, no. 4 (January 1979), pp. 417–19.

[2]Jack Cassidy and Carol Vukelich, "Survival Reading for Parents and Kids: Parent Education Program," *The Reading Teacher*, vol. 31, no. 6 (March 1978), p. 638.

- Helping them look forward to school as a happy place
- Speaking slowly and clearly and, if bilingual, showing interest in learning a new language
- Encouraging regular attendance
- Conferring frequently with the teacher concerning the children's progress
- Listening to their children read
- Using community resources to give the children experiences outside the home and school
- Spending quality time with each of their children
- Providing a time and place for study
- Making good use of the public library

GENERAL WAYS PARENTS CAN HELP IN THE SCHOOLROOM

There are many opportunities for parents to assume responsibility, particularly in the early primary grades.

- They may oversee a group period while the teacher is helping individual children, and vice versa.
- They may help in decorating the room for holidays and special occasions.
- They may straighten shelves and encourage children to put back materials where they found them.
- They may serve on a telephone committee and call other parents regarding meetings and projects. This service will alleviate the number of notes to be sent home.
- After the teacher has written a child's name on a 4-inch × 9-inch piece of tagboard, parents may cover the name with acetate. Each child can then practice tracing his or her name with crayon. A tissue is used for erasing. These name tags may be used over and over at home.
- Parents may paint wooden coat hangers and write children's first name and the initial of their last name on the hangers using the form of manuscript letters being taught.
- They may arrange books on the reading table.
- They may reinforce the reading or phonics lesson on the days when teachers give them duplicated copies or books to take home and use.
- They may serve as listeners in the classroom so each child will have many opportunities to read aloud.
- They should be invited to observe the teacher instructing the children in reading and phonics.

○ They should be encouraged to tell other parents of their own experiences in the reading program.

Usually parents will respond eagerly to a program that welcomes their participation. If they feel a part of the program, they will be more likely to attend meetings and confer with the teacher.

SPECIAL VISUAL MATERIALS THAT CAN BE MADE OR USED

Odds-and-Ends Boxes

These boxes can be used in many activities involving creativity, including the other visual materials described below. Cover the sides of the boxes with bright-colored contact paper. Boxes can be labeled *ABC*, *DEF*, and so on. Consider special boxes for dress-up clothes, yardage, and containers; you can use small plastic bags as containers for seeds, sequins, popcorn, and small decorations and muffin tins to hold tiny objects.

Aides or parents can make the boxes and help fill them with articles. Alphabet boxes may be used for the following items, none of which contains a consonant blend or a digraph in its name. Encourage children to add to the collection.

A: acorns, plastic alphabet letters
B: balloons, bottles (plastic), burlap, buttons, birthday cards, bags (paper), boxes (different sizes), balls (varied sizes), bark, beans, bells
C: candles, corn (grains), cotton, comb, candy (wrapped), corks
D: denim, dominoes, disk, dime, small doll
E: egg cartons, eggshells, plastic letter *L* ("ell"), toy engine
F: feathers, felt pieces, foil, fur, fan, nail file, four or five plastic numerals
G: gingham, goggles, games, gourd, gum
H: handkerchiefs, hangers, doll hats, handles, hook, toy hammer, heart
I: IBM cards, ice cream sticks, inner-tube rubber, empty ink pen
J: jacks, jars, jewelry, jigsaw puzzle, jew's harp, jump rope
K: kerchiefs, keys, kite, ketchup bottle, toy kettle
L: laces, lids (different sizes), pressed leaves, leather, lemon rind, letters with cancelled stamps
M: magnet, magnifying glass, mirror, play money, mittens, map, milk carton
N: necklaces, net, newspaper, nuts, nail, napkin, needle in plastic bag
O: oatmeal flakes, olives (in jar), octagon shape

P: pipe cleaners, popped popcorn, penny, pebbles, package, paintbrush
Q: quarter, doll quilt, quoits, plastic question mark
R: rickrack, rings, rocks, rubber bands, ruler, ribbons (different colors and lengths)
S: salt (in shaker), sandpaper, sequins, seeds (prune, pumpkin, peach), socks
T: tape, tongue depressor, top, telegram, tacks in plastic bag, teaspoon
U: United States (map), doll umbrella
V: valentine, visor, velvet, plastic vegetables, vests for buttoning
W: washers, wishbone, wool, wigs
Y: yardage, yarn (different colors and lengths), yo-yo
Z: zippers, Z (plastic)

Flannel Board

For mounting pictures, secure an artist's board or a rectangle of heavy cardboard and a yard of outing flannel. The flannel can be any color or may be dyed dark green, brown, or black. It should be at least 4 inches longer and 4 inches wider than the board over which it is stretched. Secure the raw edges and corners with masking tape, which can be removed when the material needs to be laundered. Outing flannel is more effective than felt, since it has more nap to which pictures can adhere. The pictures, of course, must be backed with bits of felt, flannel, sandpaper, or flocked paper.

Magnetic Board

Provide a sheet of screen and fasten it to cardboard with tape to cover the rough edges. Lay outing flannel over the screen and secure the edges at the back. Magnets can be purchased from a hardware store and taped to pictures, which will then adhere to the board.

"Feel" Book

Tie squares of heavy tagboard together with shoestrings to make a book. Punch holes through which the strings can be drawn. Glue an attractive picture on the outside of the book. Collect fabrics and articles that can be glued to the pages and that children can touch and identify: velvet, sandpaper, foil, small mirror, zipper that a child can zip up and down, gingham, denim, a flat lid, buttonholes through which buttons can be inserted, a piece of rubber, a flat shoe shape with holes through which children can lace the shoe with shoestrings, a flat pair of blunt scissors, a closed safety pin, a clothespin, and other objects that will spark conversation. The odds-and-ends boxes can be a source for these items.

Outing-Flannel Charts

Use a yard of pastel-colored outing flannel. Cut the edges with pinking shears so the cloth will not ravel. Draw horizontal guidelines about a half inch apart with a pencil and yardstick. Cut small pictures of people, places, and objects from picture dictionaries or discarded workbooks; be sure pictures are about the same size. The name for each picture will begin with a single consonant and short vowel. The pictures can be glued in two columns, 13 pictures to a column. With a felt-tip pen, write the upper- and lower-case initial letter beside each picture. This chart can be folded and placed on a supply shelf when not in use. A window shade may be used in the same manner and later rolled up and stored.

Cassette Recordings

Use a recorder, and tape the children's speech and reading to be played back. This activity will provide the class with numerous opportunities to develop listening skills.

Surprise Box

Decorate a box with crepe paper. Cover with a lid. Place a different object in the box each day. Before dismissal or before recess, ask children to guess what is in the surprise box, telling them the initial letter with which the "surprise" begins. Give enough clues so someone will guess. Try to vary the initial consonants.

Shopping Bag

The children bring in labels from boxes, cans, or packages and drop them into a shopping bag. Once a week children sort out the labels for a supermarket scrapbook and paste them in ABC order.

Directional Cards

Write directions on rectangular strips of tagboard. The teacher holds up one card. Children read the directions and respond nonverbally.

Listen.	Line up for recess.	Line up for the bus.
Stop work.	Line up to go home.	Clear your desk.
Sit.	Get coats.	Come to the desk.
Stand.	Who needs help?	Resting time.
Quiet.	Time for reading.	Time for singing.

Word Charts

Ask the children to collect pictures from discarded ABC books, catalogs, or magazines. From this collection, choose pictures that are uniform in size and paste each one at the top of a strip of tagboard. Each picture selected should begin with a consonant letter. Write the word for the picture at the top and several words underneath that begin with the same sound. The teacher may write the words first separately so they can be traced by the aide onto the tagboard. Punch holes in the tagboard strips and insert rings so the charts can be hung on a rack. Add one word a day.

Apron

Use plain, sturdy, unbleached muslin for making an apron. Stitch on eight pockets of different colors: blue, yellow, red, green, orange, purple or violet, brown, and pink. Small objects whose names begin with specific sounds can be placed in the pockets also. Wear the apron. If a child knows the color name and can say it, he or she places a piece of felt of the same color in the correct pocket. Have plenty of felt shapes available: squares, triangles, half circles, circles, rectangles, and ellipses (ovals). The child not only can choose a color but also can name the shape. Listen for *r* and *l* since most color names (yellow, blue, green, red, purple or violet, orange) have these sounds. Listen for the sound of *s* in *square, ellipse,* and *circle.*

Scrapbook

Use substantial tagboard or heavy wrapping paper for pages. Cut pictures from magazines. The names for the pictures should begin with simple letter sounds. Do not use pictures if their names begin with consonant blends or consonant digraphs. Write capital and lower-case letters at the left of each page: *T-t, F-f,* and so on. Paste the appropriate picture beside each pair of letters.

Balloon Words

Blow up a balloon and tie it securely at the end. Write a pair of capital and lower-case letters around the balloon with a black felt-tip pen. Ask children to name words that begin with the letter sounds. Have enough balloons to accommodate all letters except *q* and *x*.

Pictures for Consonant Blends—Grades 3, 4, and Advanced

Look through magazines to find pictures whose names begin with consonant blends. Mount them on squares of tagboard of uniform size. Suggestions for pictures:

bl and *br:*   blender, block, bricks, bread, brush, broom
cl and *cr:*   clown, clock, crown, crow, cross, crackers
pl and *pr:*   plane, plate, plums, present, prunes
dr: drum, dress, dresser
fl and *fr:*   flat, flowers, fly, flute, frog, frame
tr and *tw:*   tree, tray, tricycle, trap, twine, twins, twelve
sl and *st:*   sled, slide, slacks, stone, steps, stop light, star
sn and *sk:*   snake, snow, snail, skunk, skis, skates, skeleton
sm and *squ:*   smile, smoke, smock, square, squirrel, squash
sp and *sw:*   spoon, spool, spider, sweater, swimsuit, swing

Explain that *q* and *u* are almost always used together. Teach *sc* and *sk* separately so as not to confuse their spellings.

Parade of Letters

The children hold alphabet letters made of felt or plastic. Play a march. *A* and *a* take hands and march around the room. When they arrive at a certain spot, *B* and *b* join them. The march continues until all letters are in the parade. Use groups of children for this activity. It is unlikely that a class would have 52 members.

Consonant Bags

Secure number 6 bags. On the front of each paper bag, glue a picture and write its beginning letter in capital and lower-case with a felt-tip pen. Tape the bags along the edge of the chalkboard or a table. Children find pictures in discarded workbooks or catalogs, cut them out, and drop them into the correct bag (the picture need not match that on the bag, but the initial letter of its name must be the same). Once a week, someone may remove the pictures from one bag and say their names.

Yarn Letters

Display capital and lower-case letter forms in the room to serve as models. Cut strips of yarn of different colors and lengths. Children arrange the strips on the flannel board in the form of alphabet letters.

Puppets and Masks

The odds-and-ends boxes will serve well in the making of varieties of puppets and masks. Children may be shown models of puppets and then be allowed to construct their own. Aides, by following directions, can make many patterns for the children to trace. The children will enjoy projecting their voices into the puppets as they name words beginning with a particular sound, read poems, and perform many other activities in this book.

STYROFOAM CAT PUPPET

Use a styrofoam ball for the head. Construction paper eyes and mouth may be added, or use buttons for features. Add toothpicks for whiskers and attach triangular felt ears with tape. Cut a hole at the bottom into which a small apothecary bottle can be inserted. The child can insert a finger and use the construction as a finger puppet, or push in a pencil or dowel stick and use it as a stick puppet. If a garment is to be added, use the suggestion given with the ghost puppet on page 24 and glue or tie the neck of the garment to the neck of the bottle. A roll of heavy cardboard may be substituted for the bottle.

CHICKEN

Cut the body and head from a plastic sponge. Glue the head to the body. Add a tail and beak cut from construction paper. Use pipe cleaners for feet.

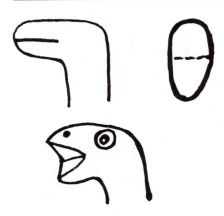

SNAKE SOCK PUPPET

Cut a slit in the toe of a sock. Cut an oval piece of red felt. Fold it in the center. Insert the felt in the slit and sew it in securely. Add buttons for nose and eye.

BEAR

Use brown construction paper for the head. Add two brown felt ears. Glue the face to a tongue depressor. Draw in features with a felt-tip pen.

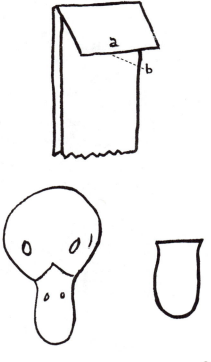

DUCK SACK PUPPET

Use a number 6 grocery bag. Make a duck head from two pieces of construction paper. Glue the main head shape to the bottom of the bag (a) so that the bill extends over the flap made when the bag is folded. The duck's lower bill must be glued to the side of the bag beneath the flap (b) so that it matches the upper bill. Show child how to place hand inside bag, inserting fingers into flap and pressing thumb against lower bill. When the flap is manipulated, the duck will appear to be talking.

GHOST PUPPET

On construction paper draw the shape of a ghost a little larger than a child's hand. Lay it on white sheeting and trace around it with a crayon. Cut two identical shapes of the ghost. Sew them together, leaving the bottom open so a hand can be inserted. Stuff the head with tissue paper and tie the neck loosely enough to insert a pointer finger. The middle finger and thumb are placed in the arm areas. Add features with a pen.

CAT MASK

From a large paper sack, make a cat mask that will fit over a child's head. Cut a hole through which the child can extend the nose and breathe easily. Cut out ovals for eyes. Use pipe cleaners for whiskers. The mask can be used for Halloween. When they wear the mask, tell the children that they must make up some complete sentences about Halloween.

BALLOON PUPPET

Blow up a balloon and tie it securely at the end. Cover the balloon with layers of paper toweling strips dipped in liquid starch. Add yarn for hair and draw features. When the outside is dry, the balloon can be deflated and the puppet will keep its shape. Cut a hole at the bottom large enough to fit in an apothecary bottle or a roll of cardboard large enough to insert the pointer finger. Drape a piece of cloth for a garment.

COW MASK

Choose a large enough paper
bag to be hung over the child's
face like a feed bag and held on
with string. The bottom of the
bag forms the cow's nose.
Construction-paper ears, horns,
and nostrils are attached with
glue. Eyeholes are cut out. The
top of the sack needs to be cut
as shown to fit over the child's
neck.

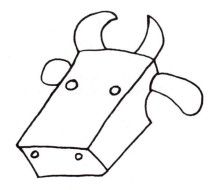

CHILDREN'S NAMES

Alphabetizing Children's Names

Most children are interested in the sounds with which their names begin.
Teachers and parents can prepare a large vertical list of alphabet letters on
a sheet of newsprint. (The teacher may write the manuscript letters in
pencil, and the aide can go over them with crayon or a watercolor felt
pen.) Each child can decide if his or her name belongs beside a certain
letter. There may be several first names beginning with B, for example,
whereas probably no one's name will begin with letters like Q, Y, or Z.
Children can exchange comments and become familiar with their friends'
names. They may ask, "How far down the alphabet is your name?"
"Which names does your name come between?" "Is your name near the
top or bottom of the list?" "Whose name begins like mine?" "Is my name
the only one beginning with that letter?" The children can begin to appreciate the idea of classifying words and will understand the usefulness of
the "alphabet ladder." This activity may lead to making a telephone book
or dictionary.

Listing Pupils According
to Names

Aides and paraprofessionals should use the class roll and learn how to
write the pupils' names in manuscript, using both capital and lower-case
forms correctly. The children's names can be the basis for exercises in
learning initial letters.

○ List pupils whose names begin like colors.
○ List girls whose names begin like boys' names.
○ List last names that begin the same.
○ List first names that begin like the months.
○ List first names that have fewer than six letters.
○ List first names that are the shortest ones in the class.
○ List first names that are the longest ones in the class.
○ List first names that begin with the same initial letter sound as a vegetable.

Name Cards

The most important word for any person is one's name. The child's name usually is the first word he or she is likely to recognize and write. Labels bearing the child's name can be prepared on the first day of school. The parent or aide must be sure to use manuscript writing, *not* all capitals. Names may be written first by the teacher and traced by the aide or parent. These names may be written on a folded card that can stand on the table or desk, or on a disk with a loop that can be hung on a hook. The name cards can be used easily to check how many children are present, how many have brown eyes, how many are wearing blue, and so on.

Name Books

Upon entering school, each child can be presented with a book of plain pages, with the child's name written large and clearly at the top of each page for the child to trace with a crayon. Say: "This is your book. No one else may write in it. You can write letters or make drawings under your name."

Children's pictures can be taken as they are engaged in various activities. These likenesses may be pasted in the book. Children may draw their own faces or pictures of their families to add to their personal book. The teacher will give copies of their own dictated stories to add to the pages. With ingenuity parents can devise many other ideas for use of the personal book.

Typing Pupils' Own Names

A primary typewriter will be useful. If the children have learned to write their names, they can print them on the typewriter, cut them in strips, and add the names to their personal books. Eventually they may want to type their favorite story by following the words in a book.

Name Tags

Write the child's name on a filing card and fit it into a small plastic sandwich bag. Punch two holes in the bag, draw a long strip of yarn through the see-through bag, and knot the ends. The child may wear the name tag on special occasions, such as parent visits.

III

PHONICS IN LISTENING ACTIVITIES

S ilence does not exist in a world of constant sound. Actually, we always hear sounds but we do not always listen to them, for listening is a communicative activity that must be developed. It demands controlled thinking. The whole organism listens and must develop the skill of actively tuning out extraneous sounds. Without full use of listening skills, there can be no deliberate hearing, seeing, thinking, and doing. There can be no exploration of what is essential or memory of what is important.

Listening implies the ability to withdraw from some situations in order to concentrate more effectively upon others. It involves a kind of problem-solving activity—the fixing of attention willfully upon impressions received through the senses. When there is awareness of these

28

impressions and perception of their meaning, they are recorded in the brain.

One can determine how accurately children hear and how well they read, write, and spell, but to date educators have not been able to test listening. Tulolo says that "waiting until research is definitive before teaching listening seems unfair to our present generation of elementary school children who need facility in this skill. It does not appear to be a skill acquired through random learning."[1]

Certain essential factors come into play as a child learns to listen actively, progressing from involuntary to voluntary stages of listening. Each factor, listed below, depends upon the others for its strength.

1. *Hearing.* This is essential before there can be ability to listen. Hearing and listening are not synonymous, though one is dependent upon the other. Hearing is a process by which sound waves are received and modified. To hear, one needs an ear or receiver to convey those sound waves, which move to the brain for interpretation.

2. *Motivation.* This awakens the senses and provides a reason for attention.

3. *Attention.* Deliberate attention is necessary. The teacher or parent can provide visual stimuli to help the young child concentrate and understand a phonics concept, for example, more effectively.

   Motivation and attention are necessary before children can prepare themselves for the learning process. Tulolo says that first "a teacher must establish clearly in mind the kind of listening expected, set purposes for the listening activity in advance, and communicate this to the listener."[2] Inform the group, for example, that they will listen and respond by gesture to all words that begin like *pig.* Proceed to state a list of one-syllable words, some beginning like *pig* and some not: *pan,* top, *pear, pie,* nut, *pet,* and *pail.*

4. *Understanding.* Comprehension naturally follows children's ability to translate sounds into meaning. A pleasant listening game will help children understand why they are listening. Children are more than sponges. They must be choosers in the market of human thinking, feeling, and perceiving.

5. *Interpretation.* An individual can listen for hours and hear only one idea or never consciously focus upon any idea at all. When a child begins to understand and interpret what he or she hears, then the child is able to concentrate and listen.

6. *Remembering.* If the motivation is strong, memories begin to form.

---

[1]Daniel Tulolo, "Teaching Critical Listening," *Language Arts*, December 1975, p. 1108.
[2]Daniel Tulolo, "A Cognitive Approach to Teaching Listening," *Language Arts*, March 1977, p. 70.

When children can detect similarities and differences, interpret, and give meaning and creativity to what they understand, reasoning and recall will come into play.

When phonics is being taught, children should listen intently and watch the teacher's face and lips in order to perform the activity and indicate that they have heard the phonetic sound. The aide, parent, or teacher must counteract zooming planes, buses, and trucks, streams of music, and voices emanating from television and radio through the use of planned periods of concentration.

HOW CHILDREN LISTEN

How children listen will be a determining factor in their success in school. An ability to hear oneself is of vital importance. In the young child this ability is intense. To improve any form of communication, listening to oneself is necessary, especially for those children who must master a second language or correct defective speech. Because intake and perception usually precede output, this chapter emphasizes the various types of listening.

Many factors influence the kind of listening a child uses. These factors include maturity level, emotional and physical health, intelligence, experience, interest, motivation, and room environment.

Research shows that children use one or more of the following kinds of listening:

○ *Courteous.* If there is strong motivation and interest, children may merely watch eyes, sit quietly, and listen with some degree of appreciation to music or a poem. They may listen courteously in order to have a turn to speak, since they observe that others in the group do get turns when they have followed the teacher's discourse and know what to do.
○ *Appreciative.* The motivation is so pleasant that, without being required to recall, the child will do so anyway.
○ *Creative.* During this stage a child is able to add thoughts and experiences to what is being said.
○ *Selective.* The child listens and responds to directions. Determining likenesses and differences between two speech sounds is one example of selective or purposeful listening.
○ *Reactive.* The child may add additional responses to the material. An example might be, "I can think of another word that ends like *fish*."

Teachers and parents can help children to establish better listening habits by

○ Being sure the child has no hearing loss
○ Presenting good role models
○ Giving the child eye contact
○ Getting attention
○ Using an unhurried, relaxed voice
○ Having a quiet place for children to read and do follow-up work
○ Establishing time to listen, if for only a few minutes
○ Using a variety of skills described in this book to foster better listening
○ Saying a word, phrase, or sentence only once (otherwise children realize that they do not need to listen the first time)
○ Motivating them to attend by introducing some of the listening and relaxation activities in this chapter after a period of outdoor activity, so that a period of repose is induced
○ Regaining attention

COPING WITH LISTENING PROBLEMS

Children are filled with enthusiasm and often find it hard to modify their group behavior. They should not be discouraged from talking or repressed in their eagerness to question or to contribute ideas. We should accept a certain amount of interruption. Sometimes, however, one child monopolizes. An ideal plan would be to grant this child special attention. After a few private sessions with a teacher or aide, the child may be more likely to adapt, share, and listen to others.

One should try to discover reasons for a child's poor listening behavior:

○ Is interruption common in the home?
○ Is there too much verbal competition?
○ Does the child dominate the family scene so a pattern of overassertiveness has been established?

Here are some suggestions that may help the teacher or aide to keep interruption within reasonable bounds:

○ Ask for hand raising occasionally so the teacher will know who wants to talk. Hand raising can be, however, a distracting measure: the too-eager children may wave their hands constantly, and the hesitant

31

child may refrain because more time is needed to organize his or her thoughts.

○ Establish the fact that sharing is important.
○ Provide quiet games or activities described in this chapter.
○ Ask, "How do we feel when nobody listens?" Encourage discussion.
○ Tell children to pretend to put on "their listening ears," or they can use pairs of ears made from construction paper.
○ Allow the shy child a special privilege, such as holding the phonics chart or visual aid. The reticent child may let a puppet do the talking.

There is nothing wrong with delaying gratification or encouraging children to wait their turn, as long as they do not feel punished for not listening. Children will learn to attend because it is a pleasure to do so and because they cannot help listening when there is sufficient motivation.

SETTING THE STAGE FOR LISTENING PRACTICE

One should remember that listening is hard work, for children must do at least three things when a parent or teacher speaks.

1. They must think about what is being said.
2. They must think about what has been said.
3. They must get ready for what is going to be said.

It is important, therefore, that a speaker minimize personal and environmental factors that might interfere with the listening process. Does the teacher:

○ Speak slowly and briefly and use words a child can understand?
○ Realize that "being told" is seldom synonymous with listening?
○ Present varieties of motivational techniques?
○ Use changes in pitch, loudness, and rate in her or his speech?
○ Give children time to think? One teacher uses an egg timer, and everyone has a "think time."
○ Provide a quiet room where some children are browsing through books, others looking at objects through a magnifying glass, and still others writing or drawing?
○ Let compliments fit the child? One teacher, in making a personal check, discovered that she uttered "That's good" and "That's fine" forty times during the course of three hours.
○ Make herself or himself available for listening?
○ Evaluate individual children's listening problems?

RHYMES FOR LISTENING ACTIVITIES

When a group dramatizes "Eency-Weency Spider," bodies relax and eyes sparkle. The children can make their fingers perform in dramatizing this poem. Fingers and toes are used more frequently than other parts of the body for exploration and investigation, which leads to learning. Touch is one of the important senses through which a child acquires knowledge and an image of the self as an "ego" or "person." These movements help children learn to move safely through space, and they effect the high level of muscle control required for the fine coordination of writing.

Young children especially will find pleasure in the rhymes in this unit because of the rhythms and finger action. The rhymes may be used following a period of overstimulation and will help prepare the children for the concentration needed in reading and writing.

The children will act out each rhyme as it is recited and repeat the words after you.

I HAVE HANDS—K, 1

I have hands that clap, clap, clap.
[Children act out each activity.]
I have feet that tap, tap, tap.
I have arms that reach up high.
See my fingers fly, fly, fly.

FUNNY CLOWN—K, 1

I'm a great big, floppy clown.
[Children act out each activity.]
I bend away back; I bend away down.
I make a big smile; I make a big frown.
I'm a great big, floppy clown.

I'M A LITTLE SEED—K, 1

I'm a little seed
In the earth below. [Children crouch.]
Here comes the rain [Wiggle fingers.]
To help me to grow. [Rise.]

STRETCHING—K, 1

I stretch up high and touch the clouds; [Reach to ceiling.]
I stretch out to the wall. [Hands toward wall.]

I bend way down and touch my toes, [Bend.]
And then I stand up tall. [Stand.]

GENERAL LISTENING ACTIVITIES

MUSIC FOR THE QUIET TIME

Music is a "must" in any classroom. It helps children relax and prepares them for skill subjects demanding mental and physical activity. Use recordings of restful tunes. Music boxes that play soothing tunes are also excellent. Let the children take turns playing the music boxes.

WHERE ARE THE TICK-TOCKS?—K, 1, 2

The children bury their heads in their arms on the desk. Move to a spot in the room and start the movement of a metronome. Move to another part of the room and do the same. Then say, "Wake up and tell where you heard the tick-tocks." The children point to the areas where they heard the sound.

WHAT AM I TAPPING?—K, 1, 2

Place a glass jar, a wooden box, a tin lid, a book, and a plastic toy on the desk. The children close their eyes. Tap on one of the objects with a pencil. Children open their eyes and identify the object that was tapped.

DRUM BEATS—K, 1, 2

Beat a simple rhythm on a drum. The children imitate it by tapping the same rhythm on their desks. Beat several patterns for them to imitate. Let children take turns being the leader.

FOLLOW DIRECTIONS—K, 1, 2

Use only a few children at a time for this activity. Tell them they will need to use their ears. Give them simple directions, such as: "Touch your head," "Bring me a book," or "Write your name on the chalkboard." Increase the activity from two to three, four, or five directions so the children will gain practice in listening, sequential thinking, and action.

SOUNDS WITH OBJECTS—K, 1

Use objects to make sounds for the class to discriminate:

Hitting a triangle	Snipping with scissors
Erasing the board	Rubbing sand blocks
Shutting the drawer	Tapping on a book
Whispering	Writing with chalk or a pencil
Dropping a pin	Tapping two spoons
Winding up a toy	Coughing or sneezing

LISTENING TOUR—K, 1, 2

Take the children on a "listening tour." They will listen for sounds and on returning will make a chart that includes all the things they heard make the sounds, such as a hammer, a saw, workers talking, an airplane, cars, birds singing. The children will learn to listen more carefully and become more visually observant.

LISTENING AND SPEECH READING— 1, 2, 3, 4

Speech reading (sometimes called lip reading) helps to increase attention span, promotes better listening habits, and teaches children to watch people's faces when the people are speaking. It also improves enunciation by developing an awareness of the organs that produce speech sounds. Here is a suggestion for a speech-reading activity.

Tell the children that you are going to ask them to point to various parts of the body, but that you will use no voice, so they will not be able to hear you. They must watch your lips and face as you silently recite the rhyme, and then point to the part of the body they *see* you say. Before you begin, read the rhyme aloud first so that children will know what to expect since some words are difficult to distinguish visually.

Pointing Rhyme

Point to your thumb,
Point to your toes;
Point to your shoulder,
Point to your nose;
Point to your leg,
Point to your lips;
Point to your arm,
Point to your hips.

Continue by asking children to point to their feet, ears, face, chest, mouth, cheek, fingers, and neck. You may substitute "show me" for "point to."

LISTENING POSTER—2, 3

Ask the class to help you make up some listening rules. Write them on the board or on a chart. Here are suggestions.

○ I listen.
○ I look at my friends when they talk.
○ I think about what they say.
○ I try not to interrupt.
○ I try to look friendly.

LISTEN FOR SOUNDS—K, 1, 2, 3

This activity should be used at different hours of the day in order to hear a wide variety of sounds. Open all doors and windows for about five minutes and ask the children to listen for sounds. When the listening period has ended, ask the class to tell what sounds were heard. List them on a chart and illustrate each one with a magazine picture.

LISTEN FOR THE LAST ALPHABET LETTER—K, 1, 2, 3

Say the ABCs in order, letting your voice grow weaker and weaker until it is barely audible. Stop and ask the children to tell the last letter name you said.

LISTEN FOR KEY WORDS—2, 3, 4

A key word is one that begins with a certain vowel, consonant, blend, or digraph and to which children can refer when working out a new word. Say: "I am thinking of a word that begins like *bed*. Can you think of one?" Or say: "Can you tell me a word that begins like *cat*?" Other key words may be *duck*, *fan*, *gum*, *hat*, and *jam*.

RELATE NAMES TO KEY WORDS—1, 2, 3

Teacher: "I know someone whose name begins like *jam*" (or any other key word the children have learned). *Jack* or *Jerry* may stand. Continue the activity using other key words until each child stands. If a child's name begins with a vowel, write the name on the chalkboard and discuss the sound.

A variation might be: "I see something in this room that begins like *top*." One child may touch the *table* or any other object beginning with that sound.

LISTENING FOR SPECIFIC CONSONANTS

HOW MANY WORDS?—2, 3, 4

Read a list of words, most of which will begin with a specific consonant sound. The children listen intently and make a mark on a piece of paper each time they hear a word beginning with the designated sound. Check to see if they have counted the correct number of words.

WHERE IS THE SOUND IN YOUR NAME?—2, 3, 4

Select a letter and write it on the chalkboard. Discuss its sound. Ask, "Where is the sound? Is it in your first name? In your middle name? In your last name?" Individual children respond. For more advanced children, ask, "Is the sound at the beginning of your first name? In the middle? Last? Is the sound first in your middle (last) name? In the middle? Last?"

ANIMAL CONSONANTS—2, 3, 4

Staple pictures of animals to the center of paper plates. The animals' names should begin with specific consonants:

b—bear	c—cat	d—duck	f—fish	g—goat	h—horse
j—jackal	k—kangaroo	l—lion	m—mouse	p—pig	
r—rat or rabbit	s—seal	t—tiger	w—walrus	z—zebra	

Children will probably not be familiar with any animal names beginning with *n, q, v,* or *y*.

Say a word and ask a child to hold up the picture of the animal that begins with the same consonant. For example, when you say "ran," the child holds up a picture of a rat or a rabbit.

GOSSIP GAME—K, 1, 2, 3, 4

The children sit in a circle. The teacher whispers a word beginning with a specific consonant speech sound in the ear of one child, who whispers it into the ear of the next, and so on. The last child says the word aloud.

FOLLOW DIRECTIONS—K, 1, 2

Use only a few children at a time for this activity. Give them simple directions, such as: "Touch something that begins like *chalk*" (*chair* or *chin*). "Touch something that begins like *picture*" (*pencil*, *puppet*).

SHAKE HANDS—1, 2

At the beginning of the year, ask each child to stand as you call the roll so the children can learn the names of their classmates. After a few weeks, say: "Today, when I call roll, I am going to ask you to go over and shake hands with someone whose first name starts with the same sound as yours." If there is no one else whose name begins with the sound, say a name and ask the child to shake hands with you.

LISTEN AND REMEMBER—2, 3, 4

Present the class with memory tests like the ones suggested below. At first, include only three objects for a child to recall. Select words from basal readers, and use words starting with the same consonant sound.

1. I went to the store and bought a doll, a toy dog, and a dish. I left my toy dog at the store by mistake. What did I take home? (doll and dish)
2. I went to a party. We had cake, cookies, and ice cream. I did not eat any cookies. What did I eat? (cake and ice cream)
3. I had a party and invited Ralph, Ruth, Roy, and Randy. Randy could not come. Who did come? (Ruth, Roy, and Ralph)

DISMISSAL GAME—1, 2, 3

This dismissal game can be used before recess, for lunch, or at the end of the day. Name flowers, vegetables, or foods. Each child listens for a word that has the same beginning sound as his or her name and then gets in line. Examples: potato—Peter, tulips—Tommy, roses—Ruth, soup—Sally, and so on.

WHERE IS THE SOUND?—4, ADVANCED

Read aloud a list of words containing the sound being studied. The children are to listen for the location of the sound (first, in the middle, at the end) in each word. If the sound is at the beginning of the word, they place their palms on the desk at the left side. If it is at the end of the word, they place their palms at the right side. If the sound is inside or in the middle of the word, they place their palms together at the center of the desk. Examples: *pig* (*p* is first); *apple* (*p* is in the middle); *cup* (*p* is at the end).

LISTENING FOR THE FINAL CONSONANT—2, 3, 4

Pronounce a list of one-syllable words, enunciating the final consonant sharply or plainly so it is not distorted. Be careful not to add an extra syllable, as "sa-tuh." Accentuate the vowel as the children say the words after you. Suggested words containing short vowels are:

sa-t   to-p   pi-g   su-n   te-n   bu-s   ja-m   he-n

LISTENING FOR CONSONANT DIGRAPHS

EXCHANGE SEATS—3, 4

Give each child a card containing one of the consonant digraphs, or two-letter sounds. Call out words beginning with these digraphs: *sh* (*ship* or *shell*), *ch* (*chair* or *cheese*), *th* (*thumb* or *three*), or *wh* (*wheel*). The child who is holding the digraph stands and exchanges seats with a friend whose words begins the same way. To make sure that children hear the digraph at the beginning of a word, prolong it if it is a continuant, such as *sh* or *th* are.

DIGRAPHS IN FINAL POSITION—3, 4

Read words, some ending with consonant digraphs and some not, as in the following list. Pause after each word so children can think about the last sound they heard. Ask them to raise a hand if they hear a consonant digraph at the end of the word. Explain again that a consonant digraph is a two-letter sound, and write *sh*, *ch*, and *th* (voiceless) on the board.

wi-sh	te-n	ca-sh
chur-ch	nor-th	ba-g
mu-ch	Ru-th	fi-sh
four-th	goa-t	mu-sh
wa-sh	lea-f	do-ll
be-ll	sou-th	ru-sh
di-sh	fif-th	hat-ch

RIDDLES FOR *ch*—K, 1, 2

Tell the children that each riddle can be answered with a word that begins with the *ch* sound. Ask them to hold up a thumb if they know the answer.

It has feathers. It is fluffy.   (chick)
It has a steeple.   (church)
We do this to our food.   (chew)
They are round and red and small. They are a fruit.   (cherries)
Santa climbs down it at Christmas time.   (chimney)
It is part of your face.   (chin and cheek)

This exercise will help the Spanish-speaking child who substitutes *sh* for *ch*, as in *cheap* for *sheep* and vice versa.

LISTENING FOR *th*—1, 2, 3

Teacher: "I am going to read some sentences. Each sentence will have a word that begins with the quiet *th* sound. [Make the sound in isolation, as *th* in *think*.] When I have finished reading the sentence, say the word that begins with the quiet sound. Watch to see if my tongue tip comes out a bit when I make the sound!"

Three is a number.
A cow gets *thirsty*.
See my *thumb*.
Mary sews with a *thimble*.
A *thrush* is a brown bird.

Beads go around the *throat*.
It is polite to say, "*Thank* you."
Cake batter is *thick*.
Our brains help us *think*.

LISTENING FOR CONSONANT CLUSTERS OR BLENDS

Keep a list of words beginning with blends on a wall chart for reference. Underline each blend.

THE *s* BLENDS—3, 4

Children raise a hand when they hear a word that begins with an *s* consonant blend. Alternate words so that some consecutive words will begin with blends and some will not. Children then cannot anticipate a word but must listen carefully. Children say the words after you.

spin (sp)	squirrel (squ)	swim (sw)	top	doll
sled (sl)	snow (sn)	fan	skate (sk)	smile (sm)
goat	hat	stop (st)	school (sc)	jump

THE *r* BLENDS—3, 4

Children clap once when they hear you say a word beginning with an *r* blend. Do not always have consecutive words beginning with an *r* blend. Children say the words after you.

tree (tr)	leaf	pretty (pr)	broom (br)
nut	crackers (cr)	drum (dr)	man
grapes (gr)	cat	pig	frame (fr)

THE *l* BLENDS—3, 4

Children wiggle a thumb when they hear you say a word that begins with an *l* blend. They say the words after you. Include some consecutive words that contain such *l* blends as *bl, fl, cl, sl, gl,* and *pl.* Sometimes the consecutive words should not begin with an *l* blend.

block	egg	flag	sled	pig
sled	plate	cat	blue	globe
clock	ink	glass	apple	clown

SUGGESTION FOR TEACHING SHORT VOWELS

CLUES IN A BASKET—K, 1, 2, 3, 4

Place inside a basket small toys or pictures of objects with short-vowel names. Say only the first part of the name. The children try to guess the whole name from your clue. Then take the object from the basket and pronounce the word. Explain that more than one word can begin with a particular consonant–short vowel sound.

Short *a:* *ba:* bag or rubber band   *pa:* small pan
          ca: can or candy   *sa:* sack or a Santa
          fa: fan   *ta:* thumbtack in a piece of wood
          ha: hat or hammer   *va:* valentine
          la: toy lamp   *ra:* rag or toy rabbit
Short *e:* *be:* bell or doll bed   *re:* red disk
          se: plastic numeral 7   *te:* numeral 10
          he: picture of a hen   *fe:* picture of a fence
Short *i:* *fi:* fish   *pi:* closed safety pin
          hi: picture of a hill   *si:* numeral 6
          ki: toy kitten   *zi:* zipper
          li: lid   *mi:* mitten
Short *o:* *bo:* box or bottle   *po:* pot
          do: doll   *ro:* rock
          lo: lock   *co:* cotton
Short *u:* *bu:* toy bug   *pu:* toy puppy
          cu: cup   *nu:* nut
          gu: package of gum   *ru:* rug

LISTENING FOR SHORT-VOWEL SOUNDS

VOWEL RHYMES FOR FUN—2, 3, 4

Read the jingles and ask the class to supply the missing word. A variety of vowels are included.

Short *a:*   A little gray rat
           Was chased by a _____. (cat)
Short *e:*   A plump little hen
           Lived in a _____. (pen)
Short *i:*   A fat little pig
           Was dancing a _____. (jig)
Short *o:*   It is not odd
           That peas grow in a _____. (pod)
Short *u:*   A little red bug
           Crawled under the _____. (rug)

THE SAME OR DIFFERENT?—1, 2, 3

Say two words. The children indicate whether the words are alike or different.

hot–hat   rat–rat   bit–bit
sat–bat   cot–cat   cup–cup

Use three words.

fan–fin–fun   pan–pan–pan
sat–sat–sat   run–ran–run
ten–tan–tan   bed–bed–bed

EAR-TRAINING GAME—K, 1, 2

The class is to supply the missing word in each of these couplets. The children point to or indicate the part of the body. Help children with the clues by demonstrating the action.

sand, band, land: See my right _____ .   (hand)
sum, hum, gum: Here is my _____ .   (thumb)
sips, dips, hips: I have two _____ .   (lips)
check, peck, wreck: I have just one _____ .   (neck)
pin, win, thin: I have just one _____ .   (chin)
beg, peg, keg: I wiggle one _____ .   (leg)

CONSONANT–SHORT VOWEL BLENDS—2, 3, 4

List these consonant–short vowel blends on the board and ask the children to say three-letter words that begin with the consonant–short vowel blends. Then write the last letter to complete each word. The children may give more than one ending for some of the blends.

ba	ca	fa	ha	ja	ma
pa	ra	sa	ta	be	me
se	pe	re	ge	pi	bi
di	fi	si	ho	lo	po
co	do	bu	su	gu	cu

LISTENING FOR LONG-VOWEL SOUNDS

LISTENING FOR LONG VOWELS—2, 3, 4

Children supply the rhyming word.

43

Long *e:*   I saw two feet,
    Walk down the _____ . (street)
Long *i:*   The moon gives its light,
    When it shines in the _____ . (night)
Long *o:*   I put on my coat,
    When I sail my _____ . (boat)
Long *u:*   I see a fuse,
    For a cord that we _____ . (use)

LONG VOWEL *o*—2, 3, 4

Read the poem aloud. Then write the italicized words at the end of the lines on the board in mixed order. Ask the children to supply the last word of each line as you read the poem a second time.

Go is the first part of *goat*.
Bo is the first part of *boat*.
No is the first part of *nose*.
And that's the way it goes!

Ho is the first part of *hope*.
So is the first part of *soap*.
Ro is the first part of *rose*.
And that's the way it goes!

Jo is the first part of *Joan*.
Lo is the first part of *loan*.
To is the first part of *toes*.
And that's the way it goes!

PANTOMIMING LONG AND SHORT VOWELS—3, 4

Say a word with a long vowel: *go, toe, rope, soap, joke, cone,* or *goat*. Say a word with a short vowel: *hot, cot, Don, hop, stop,* or *mop*. The class responds by spreading the hands apart if the vowel is long. If the vowel is short, they place the palms of the hands a few inches apart. Try this game with long and short *a, e,* and *i* too.

DISTINGUISHING LONG- AND SHORT-VOWEL SOUNDS—2, 3, 4

Read the words aloud after asking the children to listen for the middle vowel sounds, which will be either long or short. When they hear you say a word with a long vowel, they will tap on the desk twice. When they hear you say a word with a short vowel, they will clap once. Keep note if they follow these directions.

met–meat	same–Sam	pet–Pete	got–goat	file–fill
cut–coat	cat–Kate	pan–pane	beat–bet	net–neat
cot–cute	cut–cube	ran–rain	got–goat	feed–fed

IS IT A SHORT OR A LONG VOWEL?— 2, 3, 4

Prepare a list of words that contain short and long vowels. Tell the class that, when you read the list, they are to hold up one finger if the word has a short vowel and raise an arm if the vowel is long. This activity can be varied by asking the children to make a short pencil mark for a short vowel and a long mark for a long vowel.

You can duplicate the list so each child has a copy. Children can draw a line under words that have short vowels and a macron over those that are long.

LISTENING FOR OTHER VOWEL SOUNDS

LISTENING FOR *ar* OR *or*—3, 4

Ask the children to tap once when they hear you say a word with *ar* and clap once when they hear a word with *or*.

for	farm	or	garden
horse	north	mark	cord
card	corn	dart	hard
jar	arm	born	lard

LISTENING FOR *ow* (*ou*), *aw*, AND LONG *oo*—3, 4

Ask the children to wiggle a thumb when they hear you say a word with the *ow* sound:

cow	house	mouth	moon	saw	loud	town

Ask them to hold up a pointer finger when they hear a word with *aw*:

fall	ball	south	caught	cow	jaw	paw

Ask them to hold up a hand when they hear you say a word with a long *oo:*

moon   boat   tall   coop   now   food   hoop

RHYMES TO COMPLETE—3, 4

ow: I saw a big frown
On the face of a _____ . (clown)

aw: One time I saw
A crow that said _____ . ("Caw")

Short *oo:* Mrs. Ann Cook
Read from a _____ . (book)

Long *oo:* The ghost says, "Boo!"
The cow says, "_____ ." (Moo)

DIFFERENTIATING SHORT AND LONG *oo*—3, 4

The children tap once when they hear a word with short *oo* and twice when they hear a word with long *oo.*

hood	boot	wood
loop	good	zoo
foot	could	moo
book	coon	stood
moon	too	hook
boo	took	cook

LISTENING FOR *oy* (*oi*) AND *ow* (*ou*)—3, 4

Ask the children to clap once when they hear the *oy* diphthong in a sentence and twice when they hear *ou.* After the sentence is completed, they repeat the italicized words.

There are *boys* in this room.
A *mouse* ran across the floor.
A big boom makes a *noise.*
Each person lives in a *house.*
We put *oil* in a car.
A horn makes a *loud sound.*

LISTENING FOR SPECIAL ENDINGS

THE *es* ENDING—3, 4

The *es* ending adds a syllable to a word that ends with *x, s, z, sh,* or *ch.* Give the children practice in hearing and saying these words and listening for the sound of *z* at the end of each word.

matches	dresses	noises
witches	guesses	buses
buzzes	watches	noses
fishes	latches	glasses
ditches	bushes	boxes
bosses	bunches	dishes
catches	rushes	foxes

Ask the children to supply the last word in each couplet:

The big whale wishes
To eat little _____ .   (fishes)

Ugly old witches
Jump over _____ .   (ditches)

We all like bunches
Of grapes for our _____ .   (lunches)

A catcher catches;
A baby chick _____ .   (hatches)

PLURAL *s*—K, 1, 2, 3, 4

This exercise will be valuable for children who use the singular form of a noun when the plural is needed. Such children might say "three cat." Explain to the class that we add *s* to the end of the word if we are talking about more than one. Ask the children to repeat the words after you and listen for the sound of *s*.

rats	lamps	kites
muffs	tracks	dots
hats	grapes	maps
caps	rabbits	tacks
rocks	lips	jumps
lumps	rats	sets

47

Ask: "Would you say 'six bat' or 'six bats'? Would you say 'five cat'? or 'five cats'? Would you say 'two lock for the door'? or would you say 'two locks for the door'?"

PLURAL s WITH THE SOUND OF z—
K, 1, 2, 3, 4

If children omit plural s from words, they may be likely to omit s with the sound of z. They say these words after you if they end with the sound of z.

pigs	flags	hills
cans	lambs	hand
dogs	nut	fans
frogs	ban	pan
four	beds	doll
ears	horns	hums

Ask: "Would you say 'three frog'? 'Three frogs'? Would you say 'two hand' or 'two hands'? Would you say 'two ear' or 'two ears'? Would you say 'seven dog' or 'seven dogs'? Would you say 'one bed' or 'one beds'? Would you say 'three hens' or 'three hen'?"

SPECIFIC LISTENING COMPETENCIES

Evaluating listening skills, we may expect the children to

- Relax their bodies
- Show an awareness of other listeners
- Follow directions
- Repeat back directions
- Recall details
- Give evidence of understanding
- Observe the face of the person speaking
- Show an interest in words
- Participate with the group
- Participate individually
- Volunteer information
- Comprehend the meanings of speech sounds in names of objects and people
- Hear differences between sounds and between words
- Increase attention span

If the listening environment is appropriate, with few distractions, and the time span is correct for the grade level, listening skills will develop gradually from passive relaxation to more acute, powerful listening in which the child's attention will be focused upon details and the ability to attend will be improved.

IV
PHONICS IN SPEAKING ACTIVITIES

Children entering kindergarten may have several articulatory substitutions, omissions, or speech-sound distortions. These may continue through the middle grades and interfere with reading. The old saying that "children outgrow these speech problems" does not always hold true. The fact is, they "outlearn" them by correcting whichever problems are interfering with oral communication.

Speech and reading are intimately related, for reading is a form of language expression and a child's major first experience is oral. Hearing plays an important part in speech development. "Because of what the child listens to," says Beery, "the speech reflects the vocabulary, the usage level, and the sentence patterns of home and neighborhood."[1]

[1]Althea Beery, "Interrelationships Between Listening and Other Language Arts Areas," *Elementary English*, March 1954, p. 164.

Every word is composed of alphabet letters written from left to right in sequence. The child, when saying a word, must blend the sounds of that word in sequence. Emphasizing phonics makes learning to read easier, but the ability to hear and reproduce sounds should preface the ability to read and write words.

Speech correction and phonics are related closely and have a common ground in that both are concerned directly with speech sounds. A knowledge of speech sounds gives children clues to pronunciation of printed or written words. Children may learn to apply speech sounds to reading through personification of the speech sounds (giving the sounds character), repetition and review of speech sounds and known vocabulary words containing similar parts (key words), and rhyming of syllables or words.

The materials in this chapter are basic to auditory-visual-vocal aspects of phonics. These materials are basic to developing *phonics* as well as to speaking and using the language. The activities and lesson plans provide group or individual experiences in a controlled situation. Significantly, all stories, games, devices, poems, and general activities can be used effectively by aides or parents.

SPEECH INVOLVEMENTS

Some children have physical impairments, such as cleft palate, cleft lip (harelip), misalignment of dental structures, cerebral palsy, tongue tie, injury to the communication centers (aphasia), hearing loss, or a voice disorder. The most frequent speech problem of young children, however, is misarticulation of speech sounds, certain consonant sounds in particular. Children may substitute an incorrect speech sound for a correct one: *wed* for *red*, *fum* for *thumb*, or *dum* for *gum*. They may omit speech sounds entirely, for example, *top* for *stop*. They may add extra sounds, for example, *estop* for *stop*, *athalete* for *athlete*. They may distort the sound, for example, with a whistling *s* or *lateral lisp* (air spilling over the sides of the tongue).

DESCRIPTION OF CONSONANT SPEECH SOUNDS

The following speech sounds are described and suggestions are offered for the teacher's and parents' understanding. Lesson plans that provide practice follow these descriptions.

M-m: Voiced nasal consonant. Lips are pressed, and a hum passes through the nasal cavity as in *me*, *hammer*, and *drum*. The

Spanish-speaking child may not pronounce the sound of *m* at the end of a word. The sound may be isolated and prolonged.

N-n: Voiced nasal consonant. The tongue tip touches the ridge behind the upper teeth. It is held there and a hum passes through the nasal cavity as in *nut, banana,* and *sun.* The child may denasalize *n,* as in *do* for *new.* The sound may be isolated and prolonged.

ng: Voiced nasal. The back of the tongue is raised and held in position, and the vocal cords vibrate in a humming sound. Blockage of the nasal passages may cause *sing* to sound like *sig.*

H-h: *H* is a voiceless breath sound. *H* is never at the end of a word. Air is expelled forcefully. When attempting to isolate *h,* do not add a vowel, as "huh." The child may omit *h,* as in *at* for *hat.*

P-p: A "popping," explosive, voiceless sound. The lips are closed and air is released forcefully in *pan, apple,* and *top.* This sound is rarely mispronounced.

B-b: Pronounced the same as *p* except that it is voiced, as in *bed, table,* and *tub.* It is rarely mispronounced, although the Spanish-speaking child may substitute a modified sound of *v.*

W-w: Voiced. The lips are rounded for *oo,* which blends into the following vowel: "oo-un" (*one*), "oo-ill" (*will*). This consonant does not appear at the end of a word except as a vowel glide: *ow* (diphthong in *cow* and *ew, few*). *W* is rarely mispronounced.

F-f: Voiceless. The lower lip touches the upper teeth, and air is forced out in *fan, ruffle,* and *calf.* Errors: *p* as in *pan* for *fan; thour* for *four.*

V-v: Voiced. It is pronounced the same as *f* except that *v* is voiced in *van, oven,* and *five.* Errors: *b* for *v,* as in *balentine* for *valentine.* Spanish-speaking children may have difficulty. They are asked to start practice with *f* as in *fan* and move to *van.*

L-l: Voiced. The tip of the tongue touches the ridge behind the upper teeth. This is a continuant sound in *lamp, pillow,* and *bell.* Errors: *w* for *l* as in *wamp* for *lamp,* or *y* as *yamp.* Oriental children may say *ramp* for *lamp* and vice versa.

R-r: Voiced. The tip of the tongue curls up and back toward the roof of the mouth, and the mouth is open slightly in *rat, carrot,* and *car.* There are regional differences in pronouncing medial and final *r.* Errors: *w* for *r,* as in *wat* for *rat.* The Spanish-speaking child may trill the *r.*

T-t: Voiceless explosive. The tip of the tongue touches the ridge behind the upper teeth as air is released explosively in *tap*, *letter*, and *cat*. No articulation problem but sometimes it is omitted, as in *sof* for *soft*.

D-d: Voiced. The sound is produced intrinsically the same way as *t* except that there is vocal cord vibration in *doll*, *ladder*, and *bed*. Usually *d* presents no articulation problem.

K-k: Voiceless. The back of the tongue is pressed against the soft palate; air is quickly exploded in *key*, *basket*, and *book*. Errors: *t* for *k*, as in *take* for *cake*.

G-g: Voiced. This sound is pronounced intrinsically the same as *k*, except that it has vocal cord vibration. Words with *g* are *gum*, *tiger*, and *rug*. Error: *dum* for *gum*.

Y-y: Voiced semi-vowel. The tongue is raised to press against the sides of the teeth for *ee*, and it glides to the vowel that follows. Words are *yo-yo* and *barnyard*. It is used as a vowel in *my* and *candy*. Errors: *wewwow* for *yellow*; *lellow* for *yellow*.

Wh-wh: Voiceless consonant digraph, or two-letter sound. The lips are rounded and breath is blown out in *wheel* and *pinwheel*. Error is debatable, as a large segment of the population does not differentiate between *w* and *wh*.

S-s: Voiceless. Words: *sun*, *basket*, and *bus*. The teeth are together or slightly apart; the tongue tip is hidden; air is emitted as steam or a quiet hiss. Errors: *Tham* for *Sam* (frontal lisp), *shink* for *sink* (air slips over the sides of the tongue in a slushy sound, lateral lisp), *tink* for *sink*. The Spanish-speaking child may add *e* to a blend as in *estop* for *stop*.

Z-z: Voiced. This sound is produced almost like *s* except that it has vocal cord vibration. Words: *zoo*, *buzzard*, and *buzz*. Errors: *thoo* for *zoo* (voiced *th*); *do* for *zoo*. The Spanish-speaking child may have trouble with *zip*, *isn't*, and *pans*. The child is asked to start with a hissing "ssss" and proceed to a buzzing "zzzz" sound.

Th-th: Voiceless. Words: *thread*, *bathtub*, and *tooth*. The tongue tip is slightly protruded and may touch the upper teeth; breath is forced out quickly. Errors: *f* for *th*, as in *fum* for *thumb*. Spanish-speaking children may have trouble with this sound.

Th-th: Voiced. This sound is pronounced almost like *th* (voiceless) in *think* except that it has vocal cord vibration. Words: *them*, *father*, and *bathe*. Spanish-speaking children may have trouble with this sound. The same correction is used as for "quiet" *th*, except that it is voiced. Error: *dis* for *this*.

Sh-sh: Voiceless. Words: *shoe, wishbone,* and *dish*. The sides of the tongue are pressed against the upper teeth; lips are protruded and drawn in slightly at the corners. Air is forced out. Errors: *soo* for *shoe; too* for *shoe*. Air may spill over sides of the tongue in a slushy sound. Spanish-speaking children may say *chew* for *shoe*.

Zh-zh: Voiced. This sound is made almost like *sh* except that it has vocal cord vibration. Words: *television* and *garage*. Zh rarely appears at the beginning of a word. Correction is the same as for *sh*. Error: Sometimes *z* is substituted for *zh*, as in *garaz* for *garage*. Air may spill over the sides of the tongue in a slushy sound (lateral lisp).

Ch-ch: Voiceless. Words: *chick, hatchet,* and *watch*. The tongue tip touches the ridge behind the upper teeth for *t*, then drops down quickly for *sh*. Errors: Air may spill over the sides of the tongue in a slushy sound (lateral lisp). Spanish-speaking children may substitute *sh*, as in *shoe* for *chew; too* for *chew*.

J-j: Voiced. Words: *jam, engine,* and *bridge*. Production is the same as for *ch* except that voice is added. The tongue tip raises for *d* and drops down for *zh*. Spanish-speaking children often have difficulty with this sound. Error: *dump* for *jump*.

General Speaking Activity

MY TALKING HELPERS—K, 1, 2

Ask the children to point to the various speech helpers as you say the poem below. Then ask them to say the syllables or words with you the second time.

> My jaw moves up and down
> Just like a funny clown.
> [Move jaw up and down.]
> My teeth can bite and chew.
> They help make speech sounds too.
> [Show teeth.]
> My nose lets sounds come through,
> [Point to nose.]
> When I say *Nee-no-noo!*
> I press my lips to say,
> *Pan* and *ball* and *may.*
> [Press lips.]

My tongue tip helps me say
Tee, toe, too, tah, tay!
[Open mouth so tongue action can be seen.]
My roof is front and back,
Tick, tock, click, clock, clack!
My voice box makes a hum
When I say *fun* and *drum.*
[Prolong *n* and *m.*]

LESSON PLANS FOR TEACHING CONSONANT SPEECH SOUNDS—K, 1, 2

When helping the children produce the sounds in these lesson plans, the teacher is advised to work with the entire group, since all children can benefit from learning about the sounds they produce in words and in connected speech. Note that no consonant blends or digraphs are included. Blends are covered in subsequent chapters. You may wish to use the *Soundie Stories* along with these exercises. These plans are for instruction to the child as well as to the teacher.

Lesson Plan for *m*

Making the Sound: "Keep the lips together and hum as you say *mop, man*, and *moon*. Repeat the words after me and feel the hum. Let's say these words and listen for the hum: *mitten, moon, mop, mule; hammer* [middle]; *gum* [end]."

WORDS TO RHYME

The children repeat the rhymes after you. The second time, pause for children to supply the rhyming word.

Fan rhymes with _____ . [man]
Ten rhymes with _____ . [men]
Top rhymes with _____ . [mop]
Kitten rhymes with _____ . [mitten]

Ask the children to think of other words that begin with *m*. Write the words on the board.

HUMMINGBIRD

"Here is a poem about a hummingbird for practice on the *m* sound. Say the poem with me."

My hummingbird makes a happy sound.
Mmmmm—mmmmm—mmmmm!
[Children repeat refrain.]
She flies around, around, around.
[Repeat refrain.]
She is a helicopter clown,
[Repeat refrain.]
As she flies backward, up, and down.
[Repeat refrain.]

Write *M* and *m* on the board and draw a contour box around each letter. Call the letters *em* and say that they make the "mmmm" sound. Use the terms *capital* and *lower-case*.

Lesson Plan for *n*

Making the Sound: "Hold your tongue tip on the little shelf [alveolar ridge] behind your upper teeth. Hold it there as you make another kind of hum: 'nnnn.' Use a mirror to see that your tongue tip is in place. Say these words after me and feel the hum: *nose, nine, note, neck; banana* [middle]; *fan* [end]."

WORDS TO RHYME

The children repeat the words after you.

Tail rhymes with _____ . [nail]
Rose rhymes with _____ . [nose]
Fine rhymes with _____ . [nine]
Cut rhymes with _____ . [nut]

Use the same instructions as for the "m" sound.

MOSQUITO

"Let's be mosquitoes and hum as we say this poem."

Mosquito far away.
Nnnnn! [Faintly.]

Mosquito coming near.
Nnnnn! [Louder.]
Mosquito buzzing loudly.
Nnnnn! [Loud.]
[Clap hands.] Oh! He got away!

Write *N* and *n* on the board and draw a contour box around each one.
Write the word *nut* on the board and underline the *n*.

Lesson Plan for *ng*

Making the Sound: "Say *ring-ng-ng*. What did the back of your tongue
do? Keep it up high and hum as we say these words: *sing, sang,* and *sung*.
Did you feel the hum at the end of *sing?* Say these words after me:
tongue, lung, ring, sang, wrong; hanger [middle]." Write *sing* on the
board and underline *ng*.

ADDING *ing*

Ask children to say the last word in each line or each word that ends in
ing. Stop to allow the group to say the word, as "Shoes are for _____."

Shoes are for walking, and telephones are for talking.
Lamps are for lighting, and pencils are for writing.
Eggs are for hatching, and baseballs are for catching.
Voices are for singing, and bells are for ringing.

Lesson Plan for *h*

Making the Sound: "Hold up the palm of your hand in front of your
mouth and say *hat*. Feel a little breath blow against your palm. Say these
words after me: *hen, hum, hat, house, heel; birdhouse* [middle]."

HATS

Children color and cut out hats described in the poem, and back them
with bits of flannel to place on the flannel board as the poem is said. Write
hat on the board and underline *h*. Draw a contour box around the word
hat.

Big hats, small hats,
Short and round and tall hats.
Blue hats, green hats,
Every-color-seen hats!

57

Hats with flowers, hats with bows,
Hats with feathers, goodness knows!
I want a hat that I can use.
Tell me, which one would you choose?

Lesson Plan for *wh*

Making the Sound: "Make your lips round without a sound. Now blow! Wh——! Make a pinwheel go around without a sound: Wh——! Say these words after me and feel the "blowing" sound against the palm of your hand: *wheel, which, what, when, where; pinwheel* [middle]."

WORDS TO CHANGE

Change *feel* to _____ . (wheel)
Change *mail* to _____ . (whale)
Change *lip* to _____ . (whip)
Change *meat* to _____ . (wheat)

Write *Wh* and *wh* on the board and draw a contour box around each one. Write *wheel* and draw a line under *wh*. Pronounce the word with the class.

WHEELS

Children and adults often do not differentiate between *w* and *wh*. However, the symbol *wh* appears in children's dictionaries and must be recognized as a consonant digraph, or two-letter sound. Say, "Let's learn a poem about wheels. Say the words with me."

Wheels go turning round and round.
Wheels take airplanes off the ground.
Wheels take cars to happy places.
Wheels on bikes cause happy faces.

"What else has wheels?"

Lesson Plan for *w*

Making the Sound: "Round your lips for *oo* and say, 'Woof, woof!' Let's say these words: *wig, watch, web, window, wall; sidewalk* [middle]."

Write *W* and *w* on the board and draw a contour box around each one. Write *wig* and underline *w*. Pronounce the word with the class and feel what the lips do.

CAT ON A ROOF

"Say this poem with me."

> The puppy dog's tail went wig-wig-wag,
> And his mouth went "woof, woof, woof."
> He wigged and he wagged and
> He woofed and he woofed
> At a little white cat on the roof.

"Did you hear the difference between *woof* and *roof?* Say both words with me."

RHYMING WORDS TO CHANGE

Change *dragon* to _____ . (wagon)
Change *pig* to _____ . (wig)
Change *tall* to _____ . (wall)
Change *ring* to _____ . (wing)

Lesson Plan for *p*

Making the Sound: "Press your lips together and make them pop. Feel the air pop on the palm of your hand when you make the last sound in *top*, *cap*, and *pop*. Now say these words after me. They all have the *p* ('pea') sound: *pear, pan, pie, pet, pin; slipper* [middle]; *cup* [end]."

PETE LIKES POPCORN

The children repeat lines after you.

> Pete likes pudding.
> Pete likes pie.
> Pete likes popcorn,
> And so do I!

Children quietly whisper "p, p, p, p" and feel the puff of air on the palm of the hand. Do not add a vowel, as *puh*.

WORDS TO CHANGE

The children repeat the words after you.

Change *wig* to _____ (pig)
Change *man* to _____ (pan)

59

Change *cup* to _____. (pup)
Change *met* to _____. (pet)

Write *P* and *p* on the board and draw contour boxes around them. Write *pan* and underline *p*.

Lesson Plan for *b*

Making the Sound: "Press your lips together and say after me, *bee, boy, bah, boo!* Now, let's say some words that have the *b* ('bee') sound: *bug, bed, bee, bite, boat; zebra* [middle]; *tub* [end]."

RHYMES TO COMPLETE

Complete these rhymes using a word that starts with *b* ("bee"). Pause to allow children time to think of the rhyming word.

A pink baby pig
Is not very _____. (big)
In clover we see
A buzzing _____. (bee)
It is fun for us
To ride on a _____. (bus)

Write *B* and *b* on the board and draw a box around each one. Write *bed* and draw a line under *b*. Pronounce the word with the class and feel the "bubbling" sound.

BUBBLES

"Let's learn a poem:"

Hold your bottle near the sink
When you pour your soda drink.
Bub, bub, bubble, bubble!
[Children repeat last line.]

Lesson Plan for *t*

Making the Sound: "Your tongue tip touches the little shelf behind your upper teeth and makes a quiet ticking sound. Use no voice at all. Whisper '*t, t, t, t*' in my ear. Say these words after me: *ten, tie, toe, top, two, tick*. Did you feel the ticking sound?"

MY CLOCK

"Here is a poem we can learn."

"Tick, tock, tick, tock," [Children repeat.]
Said the little clock on the wall.
"Tock, tock, tock, tock," [Children repeat.]
Said the grandfather clock in the hall.

WORDS TO CHANGE

Change *hop* to _____ .   (top)
Change *hen* to _____ .   (ten)
Change *pie* to _____ .   (tie)
Change *back* to _____ .   (tack)

Write *T* and *t* on the board and draw contour boxes around each one. Write the word *top* and underline *t*.

Lesson Plan for *d*

Making the Sound: "Raise your tongue tip and touch the little shelf behind your upper teeth. Say these words with me and listen for the *d* sound: *deer, dish, dog, den, door.* Say these words with the *d* ('dee') sound at the end: *bed, good, head, load, mud, red.*" (The sound should not be pronounced as "duh.")

WORDS TO CHANGE

Change *fish* to _____ .   (dish)
Change *may* to _____ .   (day)
Change *ten* to _____ .   (den)
Change *four* to _____ .   (door)

THE RAIN

"Say this poem with me."

Doris likes the rain when it stops.
She likes to hear the drip, drip, drops!
Dud, dud, dud, dud! [Children repeat these syllables.]

Write *D* and *d* on the board and draw a contour box around each one. Write *doll* and underline *d*. Pronounce the word with the class and feel what the tongue tip does.

Lesson Plan for *k*

Making the Sound: "Let the back of your tongue go high in the back part of the roof of your mouth. Make a cough sound: 'k, k, k.' Let's say some words and listen for the cough sound: *king, kind, kite; basket* [middle]; *book* [end]."

WORDS TO CHANGE

Change *tea* to _____ .   (key)
Change *ring* to _____ .   (king)
Change *mite* to _____ .   (kite)
Change *hit* to _____ .   (kit)

COUGHING

"Say this poem with me."

> I ate some cake.
> A crumb went down
> Inside my throat and then
> I coughed, "K, k, k, k, k, k,"
> And coughed it up again.

Write *K* and *k* on the board and draw a contour box around each one. Write *kite* and underline *k*. Pronounce the word with the class and feel the cough sound.

Lesson Plan for *g*

Making the Sound: "Feel the sound in the back of your throat when you say 'fro-g,' 'bu-g,' 'ru-g.' Let's say these words: *gum, goat, gate, geese, good, girl; tiger* [middle]; *rug* [end]."

WORDS TO CHANGE

Change *dough* to _____ .   (go)
Change *date* to _____ .   (gate)
Change *dame* to _____ .   (game)
Change *down* to _____ .   (gown)

MY PET FROG

"Here is a poem to learn."

I love my funny, little frog.
Frog-og-og-og!
[Children repeat all refrains.]
Once he was a polliwog.
Wog-og-og-og!
Sometimes I feed my frog a bug.
Bug-ug-ug-ug!
He swallows it and says, "Glug, glug!"
Glug-ug-ug-ug!

Write *G* and *g* on the board and draw a contour box around each one. Write *gum* and underline *g*. Pronounce the word with the class and feel what the back of the tongue does.

Lesson Plan for *f*

Making the Sound: "Bite your lip softly and make a quiet ffff sound. Say these words with me and listen for the 'angry kitten' sound: *fork, fun, fish, five, four; perfume* [middle]; *calf* [end]."

WORDS TO CHANGE

Change *pan* to _____ .   (fan)
Change *wish* to _____ .   (fish)
Change *sun* to _____ .   (fun)
Change *pour* to _____ .   (four)

MY KITTEN

"Let's learn this poem."

When my kitten sees a pup,
She arches her back and her tail fluffs up!
Ffffff! [Children repeat.]

Write *F* and *f* on the board and draw a box around each one. Write *fan* and underline *f*.

Lesson Plan for *v*

Making the Sound: "Bite your lower lip softly and hum: 'vvvv.' Say these words with me and listen for the 'v' ('vee') sound: *valentine, vine, vase, vote; beaver* [middle]; *stove* [end]."

WORDS TO CHANGE

Change *man* to _____ . (van)
Change *mine* to _____ . (vine)
Change *best* to _____ . (vest)
Change *boat* to _____ . (vote)

THE LITTLE GREEN FLY

"Let's learn a poem."

> The little green fly can do tricks like a clown.
> She can walk on the ceiling without falling down.
> Vvvvvvv! [Children make sound.]

Write *V* and *v* on the board and draw a contour box around each one. Write *van* and underline *v*.

Lesson Plan for *y*

Making the Sound: "Press the sides of the tongue against the upper teeth for *ee* ('ee-es,' *yes*). Say these words with me and feel what the sides of your tongue do: *yard, yellow, yes, yo-yo; barnyard* [middle]."

WORDS TO RHYME

The children repeat the words after you.

No-no rhymes with _____ . (yo-yo)
Barn rhymes with _____ . (yarn)
Dawn rhymes with _____ . (yawn)
Guess rhymes with _____ . (yes)

YELLOW, YELLOW

Children may substitute *l* or *w* for *y*. When each question is asked, they give an affirmative response.

> Is a banana yellow, as yellow as can be? [Teacher]
> Yes, a banana is yellow and very good for me. [Children]
> Is a squash yellow, as yellow as can be? [Teacher]
> Yes, a squash is yellow and very good for me. [Children]
> Is a pear yellow, as yellow as can be? [Teacher]
> Yes, a ripe pear is yellow and very good for me. [Children]

Continue the exercise using other foods that are yellow.

Write *Y* and *y* on the board and draw a contour box around each one. Write *yam* and underline *y*. Pronounce the word with the class. Ask children to feel what the sides of the tongue do.

Lesson Plan for *l*

Making the Sound: "Your tongue tip rests on the shelf behind your upper teeth. Say 'la, la, la' with me. What did your tongue tip do? Say these words with me and feel what your tongue tip does: *lamb, leg, log, laugh, look; yellow* [middle]; *bell* [end]."

LOOK, LOOK, LOOK!

"Here is a poem we can say."

Look, look, look! What do I see? [Children repeat with you.]
I see a ladybug looking at me.
Look, look, look! What do I see? [Children repeat.]
I see a little lamb looking at me.
Look, look, look! What do I see? [Children repeat.]
I see a meadow lark looking at me.

"What did your tongue tip do when you said 'look'?"

Write *L* and *l* on the board. Draw a contour box around each one. Write *lamp* on the board and underline *l*. Say the word with the class.

Lesson Plan for *r*

Making the Sound: "Curl back the tip of the tongue. [Show by holding out the palm of the hand and curling back the fingers.] Say 'ah' and gradually let the tongue tip curl back for *r*. Say these words with me and listen for the sound of *r: rake, rug, read, rhyme; berry* [middle]; *car* [end]."

Note: Since there are regional differences in pronouncing final *r*, take this fact into consideration when asking children to make corrections.

WORDS TO CHANGE

Change *went* to _____. (rent)
Change *wed* to _____. (red)
Change *one* to _____. (run)
Change *wing* to _____. (ring)
Change *wide* to _____. (ride)
Change *wake* to _____. (rake)

Since one substitution for *r* is *w*, emphasize the contrast. A second substitution is *l*.

MORE WORDS TO CHANGE

The children repeat the words after you:

Change *led* to _____ . (red)
Change *lest* to _____ . (rest)
Change *lake* to _____ . (rake)
Change *lead* to _____ . (read)

THE ROOSTER SOUND

"Say this poem with me."

Rooster Red, Rooster Red,
What do you say when I am in bed?
"Er, er, er, er, errrr!" [Children crow.]

"Could you make the 'rooster sound'? Was it a good *r* sound, as in *run* and in *rain?*"
Write *R* and *r* on the board and draw a contour box around each one. Write the word *rat* and underline *r*.

Lesson Plan for *s*

Making the Sound: "Keep the teeth together. Hide your tongue tip and keep it from showing. Do not let it touch your teeth. 'Ssss!' Make a hissing sound. Use a mirror to watch what your speech helpers do. Say these words with me: *Santa, sand, soap, soup; ostrich* [middle]; *bus* [end]."

Discriminating *s* from *th:*   "Hold up a thumb when you hear a word that begins with *th*, and hiss, 'ssss' when you hear a word that begins with *s*."

thank–sank	sink–think	sick–thick
thumb–some	thigh–sigh	sing–thing

MY TEAKETTLE

"Here is a poem we can say."

I have a little teakettle
That sings so merrily.
"Sssss—sssss." [Children imitate.]

66

It sings and sings and then we have
Some cookies and some tea.
"Sssss—sssss!" [Children imitate.]

Write S and s on the board. Draw a contour box around each one.
Write *sun* and underline *s*. The children listen for the hissing sound.

Lesson Plan for z

Making the Sound: "It is produced like *s* except that your vocal cords
move. Buzz like a bee: 'zzzz!' Say these words with me and listen for the
'bee' sound: *zoo, zigzag, zero, zip; lizard* [middle]; *fuzz* [end]."

THE BEE

"Here is a poem to learn."

I saw a bumblebee.
It sat on my no-zzz!
[Children repeat each line that ends with *z*.]
It sat on my ear-zzz!
It sat on my toe-zzz!
It sat on my knee-zzz!
It sat on my leg-zzz!

Children point to parts of the body that are in twos, such as shoulders,
eyes, arms, fingers, and say, "Here are my _____."
Write Z and z on the board and draw a contour box around each one.
Write *zoo* and underline *z*. Pronounce the word with the class and feel the
buzz.

Lesson Plan for sh

Making the Sound: "Push out the lips and round them a little bit. Blow
softly: 'Sh!' Say these words with me and listen for the quiet 'sh' sound:
shoe, shed, shine, show, shell; flashlight [middle]; *dish* [end]."

WORDS TO CHANGE

The children repeat the words after you:

Change *sip* to _____ . (ship)
Change *said* to _____ . (shed)
Change *seat* to _____ . (sheet)
Change *Sue* to _____ . (shoe)
Change *sell* to _____ . (shell)

67

Hearing Differences Between *ch* and *sh:* Children place a finger beside the lips when they hear a word that begins with *sh*. They place a finger under the nose to prevent a sneeze when they hear a word that begins with *ch*. The second time you read this list of words, ask them to repeat the words after you:

ship–chip   chop–shop
sheep–cheep   shoe–chew
cheer–shear   sheet–cheat

THE BUS DOOR

"Here is a poem to say."

"Sh-sh-sh!" goes the door on the bus.
[Children repeat the "sh" sound each time.]
"Sh-sh-sh!" as it opens for us.
"Sh-sh-sh!" Let's step inside.
"Sh-sh-sh!" And we'll all take a ride.

Write *Sh* and *sh* on the board and draw a contour box around each one. Write *shell* on the board and underline *sh*. Pronounce the word with the class and feel what the lips do.

Lesson Plan for *ch*

Making the Sound: "Your tongue tip touches behind your upper teeth for *t* and drops down for *sh*, as *t-sh*, *t-sh*. Saying the two sounds quickly will make *ch*. Say these words with me: *cheese, chalk, chest, chin, chicken; hatchet* [middle]; *match* [end]."

WORDS TO CHANGE

Change *test* to _____ . (chest)
Change *tease* to _____ . (cheese)
Change *talk* to _____ . (chalk)
Change *time* to _____ . (chime)

KERCHOO!

"Here is a poem for us to say."

One time I caught a nasty cold,
And so I had to sneeze.

I sat in front of an electric fan,
And got it from the breeze!
Kerchoo! Kerchoo! Ch, ch!
[Children repeat last line.]

Write *Ch* and *ch* on the board and draw a contour box around each one. Write *chick* on the board and underline *ch*. Pronounce the word with the class and feel the "sneeze."

Lesson Plan for *j*

Making the Sound: "Your tongue tip touches behind your upper teeth for *d* and then drops down for *zh* (as in *measure*). Say the two sounds rapidly and you will hear 'j' as in *jam*. D is often substituted for *j*. Say these words with me: *jeep, jelly, jug, jar; pigeon* [middle]; *orange* [end]."

WORDS TO CHANGE

Change *dump* to _____ . (jump)
Change *dug* to _____ . (jug)
Change *day* to _____ . (jay)
Change *dig* to _____ . (jig)

"Children, watch your lips as you say words beginning with the *j* sound. Clap when you observe and hear the sound in the words: *June, jug, rat, four, jump, duck, jeep, jack, top, duck, juice, lamp, just, job, three.*"

JAM

"Let's learn a poem about jam."

Jam, jam upon the shelf,
[Children repeat.]
Jam, jam, just help yourself.
Choose a color that you see,
And have some bread and jam with me.

Write *J* and *j* on the board. Draw a box around each one. Write *jam* and underline *j*. Pronounce the word with the class and listen for the "j" sound.

Lesson Plan for Voiceless *th*

Making the Sound: "Use a mirror. Put out your tongue tip and say 'three.' Try it. *Thank* you! Let's say some words: *thumb, think, three, thimble; bathtub* [middle]; *teeth* [end]."

WORDS TO CHANGE

Change *sank* to _____ . (thank)
Change *sink* to _____ . (think)
Change *some* to _____ . (thumb)
Change *free* to _____ . (three)

Lesson Plan for Voiced *th*

Making the Sound: Follow same procedure as for voiceless *th*.

WORDS TO CHANGE

The children repeat after you:

Change *Dan* to _____ . (than)
Change *doze* to _____ . (those)
Change *dare* to _____ . (there)
Change *den* to _____ . (then)

A RHYMING CONSONANT TEST

For assessing the individual child's ability to produce single consonant sounds in initial, medial, and final positions, duplicate the words in table 4 for third and fourth graders. Young children will listen as you read three words that have the same rhyming consonant in them and then say the words after you. Aides can listen to each child individually. The sounds of *zh, h, ng, y,* and *w* have either no initial or no final sound in words.

PANTOMIMING ABCs

The children say the rhymes after or with you and act them out.

A: Here is an *apple* that grows on a tree. [Make circle with forefingers and thumbs.]
B: Here is a *ball* as round as can be. [Make larger circle.]

Table 4. RHYMING CONSONANTS

	INITIAL	MEDIAL	FINAL
M	a man a mop	a hammer a camel	a lamb a ham
P	a pan a pig	an apple a tepee	a pup a cup
B	a ball a bed	a table a rabbit	a tub a cub
T	a top a tie	a letter a mitten	a cat a rat
D	a doll a dish	a window a pudding	a bed a shed
N	a nut a nest	a pony a banana	a pan a fan
K	a kitten a key	a basket a package	a book a hook
G	a goat a girl	a tiger a wagon	a rug a bug
F	a fan a fish	a muffler an elephant	a chief a leaf
V	a van a vase	a seven an eleven	a hive a five
TH	a thimble a thumb	a bathtub a toothbrush	a tooth a booth
R	a ring a rat	a carrot a cherry	a four a door
S	a saw a sailor	a rooster a biscuit	a goose a moose
Z	a zebra a zoo	a razor a buzzard	some bees some trees
CH	a chicken a cheese	a hatchet a pitcher	a bench a wrench
SH	a shoe a ship	a seashell a wishbone	a dish a fish
ZH	—	a treasure	a garage
H	a hat	a henhouse	—
NG	—	a hanger	a ring
Y	a yo-yo	a barnyard	—
W	a wig	a wigwam	—

C: Here is a *cat* with a furry, soft back. [Rub one palm against the other.]

D: Here is a *duck* that says, "Quack, quack!" [Place wrists together and open and shut hands to describe a bill.]

E: Here is an *egg* the hen lays for me. [Make oval with hands.]

F: Here is a *fish* that swims in the sea. [Move one hand in a wavy motion.]

G: Here is the *gum* that we like to chew. [Movement of chewing.]

H: Here is a *hat* that is made just for you. [Hands on top of head.]

I: Here is an *igloo* of snow and of ice. [Form half circle with hands.]

J: Here is some *jam* that tastes very nice. [Smack lips.]

K: Here is a *kite* that sails out of sight. [Wave hand.]

L: Here is a *lamp* that gives a bright light. [Wiggle fingers.]

M: Here is a *moon* that shines in the sky. [Make circle.]

N: Here is a *nest* for birdies that fly. [Cup hands.]

O: Here is an *octopus* with wiggly arms. [Hold up eight fingers]

P: Here is a *pig* we see on all farms. [Children whisper "Oink, oink."]

Q: Here is a *queen* who wears a gold crown. [Hold palm in front of forehead and extend fingers above head.]

R: Here is a *rake* for when leaves tumble down. [Make fingers into claw.]

S: Here is the *sun* that warms everything. [Make large circle.]

T: Here is a *top* that spins in a ring. [Twirl finger.]

U: Here is an *umbrella* with shade for my face. [Clasp hands above head.]

V: Here is a *valentine* with ribbons and lace. [Place fingertips together and bend to form valentine.]

W: Here is a *wagon* I fill up with blocks. [Pretend to toss things into wagon.]

X: Here is the very last letter in *box*. [Cross fingers.]

Y: Here is a *yo-yo*. I'll spin it for you. [Pretend to toss up and down.]

Z: Here is a *zebra* that lives in a zoo. [Hold fingers in front of face to simulate fence.]

STORIES FOR ISOLATING THE SPEECH SOUNDS

The question arises as to whether learning the sounds of individual letters helps children to understand the reading process. No one would claim that the sound of any letter stimulates a mental image other than the shape of the letter unless dramatization and various associations are employed. On the other hand, the alphabet itself is a most forceful tool quite apart from its use in the reading process. If the sound and shape of the alphabet letter create a strong association, who is to say that they have little significance?

Astute children may become so impatient to read that they will acquire an extensive sight vocabulary at tremendous speed and feel frustrated if asked to stop and sound out a word, but other children enjoy the activity of decoding words for themselves. We should remember that the ability to synthesize sounds in the process of forming words may be useful only if a child has reached the maturity to handle this technique. One way of teaching this technique is through synthesis or isolation of the sound. Breaking down words should begin early. Children should be taught that words have heads, bodies, and tails.

f (head)   *i* (body)   *sh* (tail)   *fish*

By saying the word slowly and prolonging each sound, a child can hear all three sounds clearly.

Before we can attain phonics results and help a young child to understand the relationship of letter sound, form, and name, we should supply stimulating games, stories, and activities in which the child can participate orally and that will spark high interest. *Soundie Stories* are "fun" stories that encourage children to participate in producing and playing with sounds and words as well as help them locate errors they may be making. Speech sounds are given such personalities as the "snake" or "rooster" sound. These dramatizations are brief and will increase ability to attend. Children can recall the adventures of Soundie and retell the story, using a flannel board and pictures they themselves have drawn.

THE SOUNDIE STORIES—K, 1

Suggestions for Using the *Soundie Stories*

○ Tell a story and ask the pupils to listen.
○ Again tell the story and ask pupils to participate orally.
○ Tell a story using the flannel board. Children can draw, color, and cut out pictures. They glue bits of flannel to the backs and place the pictures on the board as the story is told.
○ Suggest that individuals select their favorite *Soundie Story* and tell it or dramatize it.
○ Bring in a "sound bag" made of cloth with a drawstring added. Ask pupils to find objects such as a *rock* for *r* or a *leaf* for *l* and drop them into the bag. Be sure the bag is large enough to hold several objects, or make several bags. Paper bags will suffice.
○ Suggest that pupils add other episodes to a story.
○ Be sure to teach the alphabet letter name along with its sound. Pro-

nounce the letter name accurately; say, for example, "bee," not "buh."

B-b: THE BUBBLING SOUND

Soundie is a little elf with a pointed nose and pointed ears. He wears a pointed cap and two pointed-toed shoes. You could probably draw a picture of Soundie. The interesting thing about Soundie is that he always carries a sound bag. When he finds a sound that is fun, he pops it into his sound bag.

One day, Soundie was thirsty. He went to the bubbling brook for a drink of water. The water was babbling and bubbling: "bub, bub, bub." [Children repeat.]

"What an interesting sound!" said Soundie, who put the sound into his sound bag at once. Then he went looking for something that begins with *b* ("bee") and has the bubbling sound. He found a *bell*, a *box*, and a *book*. [Children repeat names.] Soundie remembered that children's names sometimes begin with that bubbling sound: *Betty, Barbara, Bobby,* and *Ben*. [Children repeat names.]

"Ho-hum!" yawned Soundie. "I guess I'd better find a place to sleep. Can it begin with *b*?" Where did Soundie sleep? [Children may say "bed."]

Ask: "Is the *b* sound in your name? Is there anything in this room that begins with *b* ('bee')? Look in your readers. Are there any words that begin with *b*?"

P-p: THE POPPING SOUND

Soundie wandered near a farmhouse in the fall. He peeked through an open window, and he smelled something buttery and mighty good. He heard the sound of "p, p, p, p!" [Make the sound with lips pressed. Children imitate.] What do you think it was? [Response.] It was something popping in a pan. It was—popcorn!

A white grain flew out the window right into Soundie's open mouth, and he ate it. Then he popped that "p, p, p, p" popping sound right into his sound bag. Soundie went searching for something that begins with *p* ("pea") and makes the popping sound. Can you see anything in this room Soundie might have found? [Response] He found a little *pan*, a *pencil*, and a *picture* of a *pig*.

Ask: "Does your name have the *p* sound? Is there anything else in this room that begins with *p*?" (Say the alphabet name.)

M-m: THE MOOING COW SOUND

One day, Soundie was in the pasture, when he heard a very low sound: "mmmm." Soundie looked all around and finally he saw a mother cow who had lost her calf.

"Mmmm!" mooed the cow. "My baby calf is lost."

"I will help you find your calf," said Soundie.

Soundie went to the brook and found the baby calf drinking bubbling, cool water.

"Thank you, Soundie," said Mother Cow. "How can I reward you?"

"Let me have your mooing sound to put into my sound bag so I can share your wonderful mooing sound with boys and girls at school."

"Taie it and welcome," said Mother Cow.

Soundie found some things that began with the letter *m* ("em") and the mooing sound. He found a *mitten,* a little *mop,* a *magnet,* a *milk* carton, and a *mirror.* He put them into the sound bag. Soundie took a stick and wrote capital *M* and lower-case *m* in the dirt. He now had how many sounds in his sound bag? [Response.]

Ask: "Does your name begin with that 'mmmm' sound? Is it *Mary, Mark, Mike, Millie,* or *May?* If your name has *m*, write it and show it to us."

Encourage children to find sight words in their readers that begin with *M-m* ("em").

N-n: THE SEWING MACHINE SOUND

One day, Soundie sat on the windowsill, watching a lady at her sewing machine. She was making a shirt. The sewing machine made a humming sound: "nnnn." It was such a quiet sound it almost put Soundie to sleep. Make the sound with me: "nnnn." [Children respond.]

"That's a lovely sound. I'd better grab it before the sewing machine stops sewing," said Soundie. He hurried up and popped that "nnnn" humming sound into his bag, jumped down from the windowsill, and began looking for things that began with *n* ("en") and its humming sound. He found a *nut,* a *nail,* and an old empty *nest.*

"Ha, ha!" laughed Soundie. "My *nose* begins with that sound. So does my *neck.*"

Ask: "Do you have that sound in your first, middle, or last name?" (Response.) "Is there anything in this room that begins with *n* ('en')?"

T-t: THE TICKING SOUND

Soundie has a wife. She is Mrs. Soundie. She has a pointed nose and she wears a pointed cap and pointed shoes. Soundie wears an elf suit. Mrs. Soundie wears an elf dress.

Mrs. Soundie gave her husband a watch for his birthday. Soundie was pleased as punch! He wound up the watch and put it close to his ear. The watch said, "T, t, t, t." [Do not add a vowel as in "tuh." Make the sound sharp.]

What do you think Soundie did with that sound? You guessed it! Now he had another sound for his sound bag. Mrs. Soundie helped Soundie find things that began with the "t, t, t, t" sound: a *tie*, a *teapot,* and a *top.*

"Parts of my body begin with that watch-ticking sound," said Soundie. Guess what they were. [Children respond: *teeth, toes.*] Someone's name may begin with *T* ("tee") and the ticking sound: *Tommy, Tammy,* or *Ted.*

Ask: "Is the *t* sound in your name? Is there anything in this room that begins with *t* ('tee')?"

D-d: THE DRIP-DROP SOUND

One dark and cloudy day, the rain came down. It fell in big swishes and all the animals ran for shelter. Soundie ran into the barn.

When the rain stopped, the animals and Soundie went out to see a rainbow.

Soundie heard a sound. It went "du-d, du-d, du-d." [Pronounce the *d* sound sharply at the end. Do not add a vowel as in *duh.*] You can say the drip-drop sound with Soundie. [Response.]

Queenie the duck was splashing in a puddle. "Did you hear that 'dud, dud' sound?" she asked.

"I certainly did," replied Soundie, "and I am going to put it into my sound bag right now." And he did.

Soundie made a discovery. "*Duck* begins with that dripping sound," he said. So he went looking for things that began with *d* ("dee"), which makes the new sound. He found a *dish* and a *doll.*

Ask: "Does your name begin with capital *D?* Is the *d* sound in your name? If so, write your name on the board and underline *D* and/or *d*. Is there anything in this room that begins with *d* ('dee')?"

F-f: THE FAN SOUND

Mrs. Soundie said, "It is a very warm day. I'd better get out the fan. It will keep us cool." Mrs. Soundie turned on the fan. It made a very quick "ffff" sound. [Prolong the sound but do not add a vowel.]

"What is that sound?" asked Soundie, who had big ears to catch tiny sounds perhaps we cannot hear at all.

"The fan is making a cooling-air sound," said Mrs. Soundie.

"I've never heard that sound before. I'd better put it into my sound bag and share it with boys and girls at school."

Mrs. Soundie said, "Here is a *fine fork.* And there are *five fishes* in the *fish* bowl. Those words begin with the *f* sound."

Ask: "Does your name have that ffff sound? Does it have the letter *f* ('eff')? Is there anything in this room that begins with *f* ('eff')?"

G-g: THE FROG SOUND

Soundie went exploring and met Mr. Frog down by the pond, where frogs like to be.

"I have found a new sound. And your name begins with it: 'Ffff' *frog, frog,*" said Soundie.

"Gug, gug, glug," croaked Mr. Frog. "That's a *good* sound. But the sound I make is better." Mr. Frog puffed out his throat and croaked, "Gug, gug, glug, gug." [Children imitate.] "I am a fro-g, fro-g, frog!" [Children imitate.]

"May I put that sound into my sound bag?" asked Soundie politely.

"Gug," said Mr. Frog. "Take a dozen sounds if you wish."

"One will be fine, thank you, " said Soundie.

Soundie found a package of *gum* to remind him of the frog sound.

Ask: "Does your name begin with G ('jee')? Is it *Gary?* Is the g ('jee') sound in your name?

H-h: THE PANTING SOUND

It was a very warm day. Soundie found a bush and lay down under it to take a nap. He took off his little pointed hat and laid it on the ground. When he woke up, his hat was gone.

He looked all around and finally he saw his hat. It was walking! Soundie sneaked up behind the walking hat and grabbed it. Underneath was a little puppy. It had crawled under Soundie's hat to keep cool.

"Ho, ho, ho," laughed Soundie.

The warm sun made the puppy pant, "H, h, h, h." [Do not add a vowel as in "huh."]

Soundie popped that sound right into his sound bag. It was such a quiet sound, but Soundie knew something.

"*Hat* begins with that panting sound," he said excitedly. "And parts of my body begin with the h ('aitch') sound too: *hand* and *hips* and *heart.*"

Ask: "Is the h sound in your name? Is there anything in this room that begins with h ('aitch')?"

K-k: THE COUGH SOUND

Mrs. Soundie had a tickle in her throat, and she started to cough, "K, k, k, k."

"What sound is that?" asked Soundie.

"I am coughing, so I guess it is a cough sound," she replied.

"I've never thought about that sound, although I have coughed once or twice myself," said Soundie.

"K, k, k, k," coughed Mrs. Soundie.

"Here is some lemon juice," said Soundie. "It may help your cough."

Mrs. Soundie took a teaspoonful of lemon juice, and her cough went away.

"Oh, dear!" sighed Soundie, "I wanted to catch that sound for my sound bag."

Mrs. Soundie coughed once more: "K, k, k, k!" Soundie caught the sound just in time to plop it into his sound bag. Then he found a *key* and a *kite* to remind him that *k* ("kay") makes the cough sound.

Ask: "Is there a *k* sound in your name? Is there anything in the room that begins with *k* ('kay')?"

J-j: THE JEEP SOUND

Soundie was at the farm when he saw a farmer. Soundie quickly hid behind a pile of hay because people are not supposed to see elves.

The farmer got into his jeep and tried to start it. The engine went "j, j, j, j." [Do not pronounce as *juh.*]

"The farmer has a problem," said Soundie. "I wish I could help him."

"J, j, j, j," went the stubborn engine.

"Well, I'd better pop that sound into my sound bag," said Soundie.

The farmer put some gas into the tank and drove the jeep away. Soundie went home and had some bread and *jam.*

Ask: "Is there a *j* sound in your name? Is there anything in the room that begins with *j* ('jay')?"

L-l: THE SINGING SOUND

It was fall. Leaves were turning red, brown, and gold. Soundie made a crunching sound with his little pointed shoes as he walked on the dry leaves. Wind was blowing through the trees making a singing sound: "l, l, l, l." [Children make the sound by raising the tongue tip and holding it on the ledge behind their upper teeth.] The wind seemed to be singing, "L, l, l, l, lllleaves are falling, falllling, winter is calling, calllling." [Children repeat with you.]

Soundie thought the singing wind sound was sad, but then he remembered all the nice things about winter, and Soundie put the singing sound into his sound bag.

"*Leaf* begins with the singing sound. Lllleaf," said Soundie. "I can make good use of that sound." So he found some words in a book that begin with *l* ("ell") and wrote all of them.

Write *leaf* on the board. Ask: "Is there an *l* sound in your name? Is there anything in the room that begins with *l* ('el')?"

R-r: THE ROOSTER SOUND

One morning, Soundie saw Red Rooster sitting on a fence. He was crowing, "Er, er, er, er, errr!" [Children imitate.]

"Why are you crowing, Red Rooster?" asked Soundie.

"Because I am happy. I wake people up in the morning and they do not need alarm clocks."

"Maybe some people don't want you to wake them up," said Soundie.

"Then they can turn over and go back to sleep," said Red Rooster. He crowed again: "Er, er, er, er, errr!" [Children imitate.]

"Say, that is a fine sound," said Soundie. "I'd like to have it for my sound bag. *Red Rooster* begins with your crowing sound!"

Red Rooster didn't mind sharing his sound.

"Lots of words begin with R ('ar'). It has the *rrrr* sound," said Soundie. "A color is rrrred. We rrrrake leaves." [Prolong the sound.]

Ask: "Can you think of other words that begin with the 'rooster' sound? Is your name *Ruth*, *Ralph*, *Randy*, or *Ruby?*" (Children respond.)

S-s: THE SNAKE SOUND

One day, in the meadow, Soundie heard a hissing sound: "ssss!" [Children make the sound.] Soundie peered inside a hollow stump. The sound was not there. He peeked behind the maple tree. There was Sammy Snake curled up in a ring. Then he curled into an *s* ("ess") shape like the letter *s*.

"Hi, Sammy Snake," greeted Soundie. "That is a mighty strange sound you are making."

"Yessss, I ssssuppose it is sssstrange to you," replied Sammy Snake. "But it is snake language and it doesn't ssssound sssstrange to me."

"May I have one of your sounds for my sound bag?" asked Soundie. "I know I will use it often."

"I'll ssssing a ssssong for you," said Sammy. "It is fun to ssssleep in the ssssun. Ssss!"

"Thank you for the song," said Soundie as Sammy crawled away. Soundie said, "Sammy's name begins with the *ssss* sound and *Soundie* begins with S ('ess'), too. There must be lots of words that begin with that sound."

Ask: "Is there an *s* sound in your name? Is there anything in the room that begins with *s* ('ess')?"

V-v: THE AIRPLANE SOUND

Soundie's pointed ears heard a very loud sound: "vvvv!" He bit his lip slightly and made the sound using a big voice: "Vvvv!" [Children imitate.] He made the sound again using a little, soft voice: "Vvvv!" [Children imitate.] But the sound was still there. Was it behind a bush? No. Was it in the cave at the side of a hill? No. Was it in the sky? Yes. It was flying high. It was flying low. Have you guessed? It was an *airplane.*

"How interesting," said Soundie. "I must have that sound." So Soundie put it right into his sound bag.

He wrote a big capital *V* and he made a smaller *v* ("vee"), and then he drew a *valentine* and a moving *van.* That was fun. Soundie discovered that *valentine* and *van* both began with the airplane sound. [Children repeat the words.]

Ask: "Is the *v* sound in your name? Is there anything in this room that begins with *v* ('vee')?"

W-w: THE WOOFING DOG SOUND

"Have you heard any new sounds lately?" asked Mrs. Soundie.

"Oh, I listen all the time. But I haven't heard any new sounds today."

Mrs. Soundie said, "I just heard a new sound. Listen!"

Woofie, the watchdog, was barking. "Woof, woof, woof!" She was barking at a cat on the roof. Where was the cat? [Response.] How did Woofie bark? [Response.]

"Well, said Soundie. "*Woof* begins with *w* ('double *u*'), and it is the first sound in Woofie's name. I'll put it into my sound bag."

Soundie saw something different about Mrs. Soundie. She had taken off her pointed hat and she was wearing a *wig.*

"It's the newest style," said Mrs. Soundie.

"Wear it if it makes you happy," said Soundie. "I like you whether you are wearing a wig or not."

Ask: "Is there a *w* sound in your name? Is there anything in the room that begins with *w* ('double *u*')?"

Y-y: THE YIPPY PUPPY SOUND

Soundie was walking down a path that led to the woods. He liked the woods, for they smelled of wildflowers and moss.

All at once he heard a little sound. "Yip, yip, yip!" [Children imitate.] What do you think was making that sound? [Response.] It was a little puppy.

"Why are you making that 'yip, yip' sound?" asked Soundie.

"Because I am lost. I can't find my mother," whined the little puppy. "Yip, yip, yip!"

"Who is your mother?" asked Soundie.

"Woofie, the watchdog," said the puppy.

"I will take you to your mother. But first I would like to put your 'yip, yip' sound into my sound bag."

Ask: "Is there a *y* sound in your name? Is there anything in this room that begins with *y*?" (Use the letter name.)

Z-z: THE BUMBLEBEE SOUND

Soundie spent most of his time on the farm and in the woods, but one day, Zoom, the bumblebee, flew by. It flew close to Soundie's listening ear and it buzzed loudly: "Zzzz!" [Children imitate.]

"Your sound is very loud. Please make it more softly," said Soundie.

The bumblebee buzzed, "Zzzz!" very softly. [Children imitate.]

"I'm going to the zoo," said Zoom. "Do you want to come with me?"

"Yes," said Soundie. "But you will have to fly slowly or I won't be able to keep up with you." Soon they came to the zoo.

"What kind of funny horse is that?" asked Soundie.

"That is not a horse. That is a zebra. Look at her stripes. They go around her head and body and even her tail. And she has a baby zebra that looks just like her," Zoom explained.

Zoom began to fly around and around. "Zzzz!" He buzzed close to the zebra's ear.

Swish! went the zebra's tail.

"Zzzz! Let's get out of here! I do not want to be swished by a zebra's tail," said the bumblebee.

Soundie laughed and laughed. He put the bumblebee's buzzing sound into his bag. He discovered that *zebra* begins with the buzzing sound: "zzzebra." And so does *zoo:* "zzzzoo." [Children imitate.] So it was a useful sound after all.

Ask: "Is there a *z* sound in your name? Is there anything in the room that begins with *z* ('zee')?"

Sh-sh: THE QUIET SOUND

Soundie decided to go to the beach. It was a very warm day. So Soundie tucked an umbrella under his arm, got on a bus, and traveled to the seashore.

Soundie lay on the sand and went to sleep. When he woke up, he stretched and yawned, "Ho-hum!" Then his hand touched something. It was a pretty seashell. It was a conch shell.

Soundie held it to his ear. "Sh-sh-sh," it whispered. [Children make the sound.]

"What a lovely sound," said Soundie, listening to the quiet sound. "Sh-sh-sh," whispered the seashell again. Soundie just loved that sound. He popped it

81

into his bag in a hurry. Soundie was happy about that quiet sound, so he set about finding words that begin with *sh.* He found *she, shoes, ship, shine, show,* and *shell.* [Children repeat each word slowly, listening for the *sh* sound.]

Ask: "Is there a *sh* sound in your name? Is there anything in the room that begins with *sh* ('es aitch')?"

Ch-ch: THE SNEEZE SOUND

Mrs. Soundie and Soundie went to the meadow to pick wildflowers. A little fly came buzzing by and sat on Soundie's little pointed nose. Soundie began to sneeze: "Ah-choo, ch, ch, ch!"

Mrs. Soundie gave Soundie a handkerchief so that he could hold it in front of his nose and the sneezes would not spread around.

"Ch, ch—ah—ch!" Soundie sneezed again.

Mrs. Soundie said, "That sneeze sound is a good one for your sound bag."

"Ch!" sneezed Soundie, and he put the sound right into his bag at once. The fly flew away and didn't tickle Soundie's nose any more. But now Soundie had a new sound that we hear in *cheese, chicken, children,* and *chimney.* [Children repeat words.]

Ask: "Does your name begin with a *ch* sound? Is there anything in the room that begins with *ch* ('cee-aitch')?" Spanish-speaking children may substitute *sh* for *ch* and will need added practice on the *ch* sound.

Wh-wh: THE WIND SOUND

One day, Soundie was sitting under his toadstool when he heard a very quiet sound. It was not a whistle. It was more like a whisper. Soundie listened carefully. "Wh-wh-wh-wh!" [Children imitate.] Use no voice. Make the first sound when you say *wheel.* Did you hear that quiet sound? [Children pronounce *wheel.*]

Well, Soundie discovered that wind blowing through leaves on the tree was making that sound. "Wh-wh-wh-wh!" Soundie held up the palm of his hand, and you can do that too. He said *wheel* and felt a little breeze flow against his palm: *wh-eel, wh-iskers, wh-irl, why-y.* [Children imitate.] Now Soundie had another sound for his sound bag, which was getting quite full by now. He went to find a dictionary to see if there were words that began with *wh.* There were many words.

Ask: "Does your name begin with a *wh* sound? Is there anything in the room that begins with *wh* ('double-*u* aitch')?"

Th-th (VOICELESS): GRAY GOOSE'S SOUND

Gray Goose was angry about something, so she put out her tongue and hissed: "Th-th-th-th!" [Children imitate the sound.]

"Say!" exclaimed Soundie. "That's an odd sound, Mrs. Goose."

"It's the only sound I know how to make when I am scared or angry," said Mrs. Goose.

"Well, don't be so angry. There's nothing to be scared about," said Soundie. Mrs. Goose bit Soundie on his thumb.

"Ow!" cried Soundie. "That was not a nice thing to do, Mrs. Goose. But just for that, I am going to take your sound and hide it away in my sound bag. I know there must be words that begin with that sound." So in went Mrs. Goose's sound into the sound bag, and Soundie found a lot of words that begin with the *th* sound: "*Thank* you, *think, throne, three,* and *thumb* because Gray Goose bit me on the thumb." [Children repeat words.]

Ask: "Does your name begin with the *th* sound? Is there anything in the room that begins with *th* ('tee aitch')?"

Th-th (VOICED): THE NOISY SOUND

Something made a noisy sound. It went, "Th-th-th-th." [Children imitate using voice.] It was kind of buzzing sound, and you can feel it in the lower part of your throat, as Soundie did. He put out his little tongue and said *they, the, this, that, these,* and *those.*

Of course, that is one of Soundie's special sounds because he uses those words so many times when he makes sentences.

Ng (NO STORY)

There is no Soundie Story for this final consonant digraph sound, as in *sing, long, lung,* and *hang.* Some children denasalize the sound as *sig.* Most children pronounce this sound; however, they often substitute *n* for *ng,* as in *singin'* for *singing.*

SUGGESTIONS FOR TEACHING CONSONANT DIGRAPHS

Read the poems to the class, write the italicized words on the board, and underline each digraph.

DISCOVERY—2, 3, 4

Here is something that we have found:
Two letters sometimes make just one sound.
Sh is for *shell* that I find in the sand.
Th is for *thumb* that I have on each hand.
ng is the very last sound in *ring.*
Wh is for *wheel* that turns with a zing!
Ch is for *chick* that likes the warm sun.
Th is for *they* and that means more than one.

Ch-ch and *Sh-sh* Digraphs

Ch AND *sh* MAKE JUST ONE SOUND—
2, 3, 4

C and *h* make just one sound
In *children, chick,* and *choo-choo!*
But I can hear it at the end
Of *catch* and *much* and *lunch* too.

WRITE *sh* OR *ch*—2, 3, 4

Write the incomplete words on the board. Invite volunteers to write *sh* or *ch* to complete each word. The words must make sense.

bru_____   fi_____   di_____   lun_____   ben_____
rea_____   hu_____   bea_____   pea_____   wi_____

COMPOUND WORDS WITH *sh*
OR *ch*—3, 4

Write compound words or two separate words that have *ch* or *sh* on the board. Ask children to pronounce them and use them in sentences.

chalkboard	wishbone	potato chip	seashell
T-shirt	flashlight	armchair	cheese sandwich
toolchest	fishbowl	trash can	checkerboard

ANOTHER NAME FOR IT—3, 4

Write these words on the board. Ask individual children to pronounce them. Say a word that is a synonym and ask children to say the correct word beginning with *ch*. Then ask them to complete the sentences orally using words in the list.

chuckle	cheap	chase
chat	chum	child
correct change	chop	choose

To laugh is to _____ . (chuckle)
It is not expensive. It is _____ . (cheap)
Correct money you receive is _____ . (correct change)
A pal or friend is a _____ . (chum)
To run after is to _____ . (chase)
To take is to _____ . (choose)
A very young person is a _____ . (child)
To talk is to _____ . (chat)
To cut wood is to _____ . (chop)

STILL ANOTHER NAME FOR IT—3, 4

These words begin with *sh*.

shout	sheet	shack	shake	share
short	shower	shut	shawl	shear

To cut wool off a sheep is to _____ it . (shear)
To yell is to _____ . (shout)
Rain may be a _____ . (shower)
To close is to _____ . (shut)
Not tall is _____ . (short)
To shiver is to _____ . (shake)
To give is to _____ . (share)
An old house can be a _____ . (shack)
A covering can be a _____ . (shawl)
A bed has a _____ . (sheet)

TO WHOM DOES IT BELONG?—3, 4

Duplicate the exercise and write the ten words on the board. Children read the sentence and supply the last word.

1. chicken	2. cheese	3. chair	4. checkers	5. cherry
6. chimney	7. chalk	8. cheek	9. chart	10. chips

Ask children to supply the correct word out loud.

Potatoes belong to _____ . (chips)
Feathers belong to a _____ . (chicken)
Game belongs to _____ . (checkers)
Fruit belongs to _____ . (cherry)
Words belong on a _____ . (chart)
Blackboard belongs to _____ . (chalk)
House belongs to _____ . (chimney)
Furniture may be a _____ . (chair)
Mice like _____ . (cheese)
Your face has more than one _____ . (cheek)

THE TRAIN RIDE—K, 1, 2

This story is for practice on the *ch* and *sh* speech sounds, which are particularly confusing for Spanish-speaking children.

In the amusement park, there was a little train. The bell went, "Ding, ding!" [Children repeat.] The engine went, "Choo, choo, choo!" [Children repeat.] The little train started: "Ch, ch, ch, ch, ch!" Then it slowed down and stopped: "Ch, ch, ch—sh—sh! SHHHHHH!"

A girl with a pink sweater got on. Her name was _____ . [Girl holds shoulders of boy.]

The little train picked up many passengers as it ran around the track. The children had a jolly time. But after a while they decided to go home to lunch.

Repeat the bell and engine sounds and say, "The train stopped to let _____ off." Describe any article of clothing as children get on and off the train. They move around the room saying, "Ch, ch, ch," and "Sh" when the train stops.

Th-th Digraphs

Th MAKES JUST ONE SOUND—2, 3, 4

Ask the children to let the tongue tip peek out each time they say a word with *th*. Read the rhyme to the class, write the *th* words on the board, and underline the *th* digraph.

T and *h* make just one sound
You hear in *think* and *throw*.
But you can hear it at the end,
Of *bath* and *tooth*, you know.

86

I AM THANKFUL—K, 1, 2, 3

I am thankful for toys,
I am thankful for school,
I am thankful for birds that fly,
I am thankful for flowers,
I am thankful for food,
And for airplanes that fly in the sky.

The children learn this poem and say it with you. They practice on the *th* sound in thankful. Ask them why they are thankful. Write their responses on the board.

THINKING ABOUT QUIET *th*—3, 4

Th is a voiceless two-letter sound. It is a consonant digraph produced when the tongue tip protrudes slightly between the teeth.
Write a list of words beginning with voiceless *th* on the board and ask pupils to match words that are synonyms, or have the same meanings. Then ask them to supply the last word in the sentences.

thaw	throw	throat	thrifty	throne
thump	theft	through	earth	both

A big bump is a _____ .   (thump)
A neck is a _____ .   (throat)
To toss is to _____ .   (throw)
Stealing is _____ .   (theft)
To be done is _____ .   (through)
Two means _____ .   (both)
A seat is a _____ .   (throne)
Melt means to _____ .   (thaw)
The soil means the _____ .   (earth)
To save is to be _____ .   (thrifty)

THE VOICED OR NOISY *th* SOUND—3, 4

Read the poem to the class, write the *th* words on the board, and underline the *th* digraph.

Sometimes *th* is noisy.
I see the words each day.
I see the words in my readers
Like *the* and *them* and *they*.

Ask pupils to find words in their readers that begin with noisy *th* and use them orally in sentences.

Write the following words on the board:

the   this   that   these   those   them   they   their

Duplicate this lesson, read the sentences aloud, and ask children to fill in the correct word orally.

_____ apple is good to eat.   (The, This, That)
_____ cats are my pets.   (Those, These)
_____ like milk.   (They)
_____ coats are furry.   (Their)

IN THE MIDDLE OF THE WORD—4

Listen for the voiced *th* as children pronounce these words. Ask them to use the words to complete sentences.

rhythm   weather   brother   feather   leather
clothing   bathing   breathing   southern   northern

It is cold in winter so we have snowy _____ .   (weather)
The band has _____ .   (rhythm)
Texas is in what direction as a state? (southern)
Alaska is in what direction as a state? (northern)
Your lungs are for _____ .   (breathing)
A tub is for _____ .   (bathing)
We wear _____ .   (clothing)
Chickens have more than one _____ .   (feather)
A coat may be made of _____ .   (leather)
A boy can be her _____ .   (brother)

Wh-wh Digraph

Wh MAKES JUST ONE SOUND—2, 3, 4

Read the poem aloud, write the *wh* words on the board, and underline the *wh* digraph.

W and h make just one sound
In *what* and *which*, my friend.
Wh is first in words we know,
But never at the end.

Write the question words *which*, *what*, *why*, *when*, and *where* on the board. Ask each child to make up an oral sentence using one of the words. Explain that *who* is a rebel word: it sounds like "hoo."

WHEELS—2, 3, 4

Here is a poem that will help with the *wh* consonant digraph. Children may learn to say it as a group, individually, or one line per child.

Wheels are on *wheelbarrows*,
Wheels are on planes,
Wheels are on *whirlybirds*,
Wheels are on trains
Wheels are on tractors
That help plant *wheat*.
Wheels are on trucks
That *whir* down the street.
Wheels are on *pinwheels*
That we can blow.
Wheels are *everywhere* we go.

Ask: "What else has wheels? Look in your dictionary for words that begin with *wh*. Take turns pronouncing them and listening for the first sound."

Ng Digraph

Ng MAKES JUST ONE SOUND—1, 2, 3

Read the rhyme. Encourage children to say it with you.

The letters *n* and *g*
Are made inside your nose.
Your tongue is raised high at the back,
And that's the way it goes!

THE *ng* SOUND—3, 4

The consonant *ng* is a nasal sound. Ask children to repeat the sounds bells make and to feel and hear the *ng* sound.

Wedding bells will sing a tune
On Saturdays, Sundays, and in June.
Ping, pong, ding, dong! [Children repeat.]

89

In Colonial days bells told of fear
To say that enemies were near.
Bing, bang, bong! [Children repeat.]
Big Ben in London tells the time,
And rings in deep and lovely chime.
Bong, bong, bong! [Children repeat.]
The Liberty Bell rang out, you see,
For thirteen colonies that were free.
Gong, gong, gong! [Children repeat.]
The bell buoy rings and rings and rings
To warn the ships of dangerous things.
Ding, ding, ding, ding, ding! [Children repeat.]

USING THE *ing* ENDING—2, 3, 4

Adults as well as children sometimes substitute *n* for *ng*, as in *singin'* for *singing*. Ask children to supply a word that rhymes:

The donkey is braying The children are _____ .	Brains are thinking, Eyes are _____ .
Leaves are for raking. Cakes are for _____ .	Feet are for tapping. Hands are for _____ .
Feet are kicking. Clocks are _____ .	Meat is roasting. Bread is _____ .
Flowers are growing. Roosters are _____ .	Eggs are frying. Birds are _____ .
Winter is calling. Leaves are _____ .	Bells are ringing. People are _____ .

CONSONANT BLENDS OR CLUSTERS

BLENDS IN RHYME—2, 3, 4

Review the *l*, *r*, and *s* blends. Say "b [bee] l [ell]" rather than distort the pronounciation of the blends. After one reading of the poem, the class can join in saying some of the verses. These rhymes may be written on a wall chart. Ask the children to find pictures to illustrate the words with blends.

B-l is for *block* I play with on the floor;
C-l is for *clock* that chimes half past four.

90

F-l is for *flag* that is red, white, and blue;
S-l is for *sled* that is shiny and new.
P-l is for *plate* that holds food for me;
G-l is for *globe* that shows land and sea.
B-r is for *broom* that sweeps the floor clean;
F-r is for *frog* that croaks and is green.
C-r is for *crown* a king wears on his head;
D-r is for *dress* with stripes blue and red.
G-r is for *grapes* that grow on a vine;
T-r is for *tree*, oak, maple, or pine.
P-r is for *present* I get in the mail;
S-q is for *squirrel* with a long, bushy tail.
S-t is for *star* that shines in the sky;
S-w is for *swing* that sends me up high.
S-c is for *scarf* that is worn on a head;
S-p is for *spoon* that I use when I'm fed.
S-k is for *skates* that go zip on the ice;
S-m is for *smoke* that smells very nice.
S-n is for *snake* that crawls on the ground;
Consonant blends have more than one sound.

Twenty-two children may each have a line to say. At the conclusion, review by asking individuals to name the words that begin with blends.

LISTEN FOR BLENDS—2, 3, 4

Say: "Clap once and repeat the word when you hear me say a word that begins with a consonant blend. I will say each word slowly."

bed–bread	red–Fred	skate–Kate
black–back	snow–no	stop–top
slip–lip	ant–plant	rain–train

NAMES BEGINNING WITH BLENDS—
2, 3, 4

Write a list of consonant blends on the board. Ask: "Does your name begin with one of these blends? Say your name and tell how it begins. (*Blanche, Frances*). Does your middle or last name begin with a blend? Is there anything in this room that begins with a blend? Point to it and name it."

COMPLETE THE RHYME—2, 3, 4

Children supply orally the word that rhymes in each couplet.

It says, "Tick-tock."
It is a _____ . (clock)

Our feet we tap.
Our hands we _____ . (clap)

The food we ate
On our dinner _____ . (plate)

In autumn we see
Brown leaves on a _____ . (tree)

Up in the sky
Airplanes _____ . (fly)

A baby wears a bib
And sleeps in a _____ . (crib)

PRACTICE FOR CONSONANT BLENDS

CLOWNS—K, 1, 2

For the *cl* consonant blend, say this poem with the class. Then ask: "What else can a clown do? Did you feel both the *c* and the *l* sound as you said *clown* and *clap*? What clothes does a clown wear? In what way is a clown clever?" Say: "I am going to listen for *l* in *laugh* and *like* as well as the *c-l* blend in *clown*."

When naming a blend, use alphabet letters, "be-el." Do not pronounce the blend in isolation.

Clowns do tricks to make me laugh.
I saw one ride a tall giraffe.
Clap, clap, clap! I like the clowns.
[Children repeat refrain.]

They have no hair upon their head.
They wear a nose that's round and red.
Clap, clap, clap! I like the clowns.
[Children repeat refrain.]

DRIPPITY DROP—K, 1, 2

This poem is for practice on the *dr* blend. Children say the refrain with you. Say: "I am going to listen for 'rrrr' in *drip*, *drippity*, *drop*, and *raindrops*."

On sidewalk and street the raindrops hop!
Drip, drip, drippity, drop!
Drippity, drippity, drip!
I must be careful so I won't slip.
Drip, drip, drippity, drop!
Drippity, drippity, drip!

THE BULLFROG—2, 3, 4

This rhyme provides practice on the *gl* consonant blend and the nasal *m*. Children make the "frog" sounds with you.

An old green bullfrog lives in a pool.
He swims around all day.
He sleeps sometimes on a white lily pad.
And at night he sings this way:
Glummm, glummm, glummm!
Glug!

THE *s* BLENDS—2, 3, 4

Tell the class that each of these riddles can be answered by a word with an *s* blend. More mature children can make up their own riddles with words that begin with *s* blends. Call the letter "ess."

It is something you wear on a chilly day.   (sweater)
It has a bushy tail and lives in a tree.   (squirrel)
A red light tells us to _____ .   (stop)
I use it when I eat.   (spoon)
It is white and makes drifts.   (snow)
We use it to slide down a hill.   (sled)
We use them on ice.   (skates)
It comes from a chimney.   (smoke)
We do this in the water.   (swim)

ORAL PRACTICE WITH VOWELS

COMPLETE RHYMES WITH SHORT VOWELS—2, 3, 4

A big black cat
Was chased by a _____ .   (rat)

A hen stretches her neck
When she wants to _____ .   (peck)

It is lots of fun
To jump and _____ .   (run)

We put a snack
Inside a _____ .   (sack)

COMPLETE RHYMES WITH LONG
VOWELS—2, 3, 4

You will have to reach
To get a ripe _____ .   (peach)

Yesterday I wore
A coat to the _____ .   (store)

By the lake
I saw a little _____ .   (snake)

I use my nose
To smell a _____ .   (rose)

PUPILS' NAMES—K, 1, 2, 3, 4

Repeat slowly the names of pupils in the class after you have asked them to listen carefully for the vowel sounds in their names. Say: "This time I will say only the first part of your name. If you recognize your name, stand."

Fre (Fred)	Bo (Bobby)	Sa (Sally)
Ka (Kathy)	Ji (Jim)	Te (Ted)

Say: "This time I will say names of animals or objects. Finish the word. There can be more than one response."

Short *i:*	fi (fish)	zi (zipper)
	pi (pin)	mi (mitten)
Short *o:*	bo (bottle, box)	ro (rock)
	clo (clock)	so (sock)
Short *u:*	bu (bug)	du (duck)
	nu (nut)	pu (pup)

SAY WORDS WITH *aw*—2, 3, 4

Ask the children to guess these riddles. The answer must have the *aw* sound:

It is part of your face.   (jaw)
It is something we obey.   (law)
It is on a bear's foot.   (claw)
It is on a dog's foot.   (paw)
It cuts wood in two.   (saw)

SAY WORDS WITH *ar*—2, 3, 4

Our blue car
Takes us very _____. (far)

Out in the park
We heard a dog _____. (bark)

Bring socks to darn
With yellow _____. (yarn)

The meat we will carve,
And we will not _____. (starve)

RECOGNIZE THE *or* SOUND—2, 3, 4

Read the rhymes. Ask the children to listen for words with *or* and to name them after hearing the poems read twice.

George played an organ.
For a tape recorder.
George painted a picture
With an orange border.

One morning, I was playing.
I went to get some corn.
And in the corner of a crib,
Some baby mice were born.

LISTEN FOR *oo* AS IN *MOON*—2, 3, 4

Have the children say the word with long *oo* that completes each rhyme.

We can't see the moon
At twelve o'clock _____. (noon)

She took a broom
And swept the _____. (room)

On the way to school,
We yelled, "April _____!" (fool)

A kangaroo
Lives at the ———. (zoo)

LISTEN FOR *oo* AS IN *BOOK*—2, 3, 4

"Answer each riddle with words that have short *oo* as in *book.*"

We hang things on it.   (hook)
She makes pies.   (cook)
They are good to eat with milk.   (cookies)
We chop it for the fireplace.   (wood)

SAY WORDS WITH *ou*—2, 3, 4

Tell children that their answers will have to have the *ou* sound.

It is a place to live.   (house)
It has a long tail,   (mouse)
It is an animal that hoots.   (owl)
It is an animal that gives milk.   (cow)
It is the opposite of quiet.   (loud)

SAY WORDS WITH *oi*—2, 3, 4

It is the opposite of sadness.   (joy)
It is the opposite of girl.   (boy)

V

PHONICS IN READING ACTIVITIES

Starting to school is synonymous with learning to read, and teachers will capitalize upon this interest as they help children acquaint themselves with preparatory skills for decoding unfamiliar words. The children have entered an important period in life. The treasures of history are being offered in the form of written records of mankind. Imagination soars with tales of fantasy and adventure. Much of the future rests upon this newly acquired ability to discover meaning from a page, with its abstract symbols. Children bring to this period eagerness, curiosity, and a desire to read.

PREPARATION FOR READING

Young people are surrounded by words from birth, but only as they begin to understand them do the words mean anything. Words are adopted as the children develop the idea or concept the words symbolize. Children know about "softness" before they use the word *soft* to label an idea. This label gathers meaning as a result of further experiences. The environment provides a vast opportunity of verbal experiences. Without the help of an adult, however, much of what is available may never become a reality.

From the start, adults can help children to observe, to listen, and to feel. Children draw meaning from experiences with reality; however, one of the richest sources for learning words is pictures, stories, poems, and books shared with adults in a variety of ways.

APPROACHES TO READING

Children do not read by using only one part of the body or by learning to sound words. More than one of the following approaches should be employed.

○ Auditory skills increase attention span and develop ability to differentiate words and sounds.
○ Speech sounds create an awareness of spoken units in words and serve children when they read orally.
○ Visual skills pertain to seeing letter forms accurately. Likenesses and differences help a child to recall a word.
○ Structural analysis refers to the form of a word. Discovery in structural analysis will take place as the teacher organizes the materials and integrates them in the daily program.
○ Contextual practice helps the word fall into place within a phrase or sentence. Children use deductive reasoning by relating the word part to the whole, and they draw conclusions from the associations they learn. They use inductive reasoning to decide if a word fits the context.
○ Tactile experiences make use of the muscles of fingers and hand in the process of encoding.

HOW CHILDREN LEARN PHONICS

Children acquire the ability to use phonics by

○ Comparing one letter or word with another
○ Differentiating or contrasting one sound or combination of sounds with others
○ Classifying letter sounds and showing the relationship between graphemes and phonemes
○ Generalizing inferences and applying certain rules
○ Categorizing by learning the terminology

○   Grouping and labeling words that have similar parts
○   Interpreting through making inferences and using trial and error

When asked, "How do you read?" one child responded, "When I read, I look at words on the page all in a row and they make me hear words in my head, and that makes me think." That child was not far from the mark.

READING AND PHONICS

Buswell says, "Reading is not a process of rapid recognition of one word after another. Rather, it is a process of fusing single words into a sequence of meaning."[1] The total act of reading is therefore a combination of the visual recognition of words and the central thought processes.

Reading is only one form of communication, a single aspect of the child's language education. In the early years, the use of the spoken word is of far greater importance than familiarity with print. The child should understand print as one mode of speech, but until the many concepts of the spoken word are well established, children will be unable to grasp the concept of reading, a complex and highly systematized skill.

Although research cannot offer a golden route to success, real progress is being made toward understanding the complexity of the reading process. There is general agreement that merely learning a stock of whole words is not the answer. At the same time, certain service words such as *a, the, and, an,* and *of* must be memorized. Many children are unable to memorize enough words to fulfill their reading needs. A system of phonics is necessary to give children word power.

Since reading is a thinking process that requires the physical skills of perceiving and interpreting, the approach cannot involve mere mechanics. If the child must pause to "sound out" every other word, the mechanics have not succeeded. If used with understanding, phonics will consolidate the communication skills of listening, speaking, reading, and writing, providing children with interesting and enjoyable motivation for all learning activities. The challenge for teachers and parents is to stimulate children in such a way that they themselves feel their need to read and demand this learning experience.

PLANNING FOR READING

The early stages of the reading program should be planned carefully, with children being led into phonics in a pleasurable way, one step at a time,

---

[1]Guy T. Buswell, "The Process of Reading," *The Reading Teacher*, December 1959, p. 109.

without anxiety. Then most of them can build sight vocabulary at a reasonable rate.

Alongside the "look-say," whole-word memorization approach, children are also being introduced to phonics. If a plateau in the recognition of sight words is reached, children are likely to become frustrated. A more intense and formal phonics approach may be needed to provide them with a set of skills enabling them to decode words.

Planning phonics practice in small steps and with frequent review before a child reads is more effective than all the remedial activities in the world. Mushrooms attain growth overnight; redwood trees require decades to attain full stature. Time was required for children to mature to a point where they could listen and manipulate the speech mechanism. To read well is to progress slowly, carefully, and consistently. In addition, emphasis upon quick achievement may devalue the warm contacts of teaching.

A CHILD'S MASTERY
OF PHONICS

From the moment children know that a bed is for sleeping, and can say *bed* and *sleep*, they are learning the art of blending sounds to form words. This is the substance of phonics. Just as musical notes are learned and blended into song, so are speech sounds blended into complete, meaningful wholes called *words*. As soon as children have mastered simple phonics principles, such as seeing similarities among initial letter sounds, and can recall key words that will be constant, lasting friends, they have taken one step toward word mastery. When they have acquired five short vowels, another step has been taken. When they see consonant blends and digraphs as units, further strength has been gained. And so children progress through steps of mastering more and more phonics concepts. The children have developed a sequence of ideas that involve meaningful integration of all communication skills.

This chapter describes a decoding system and offers many activities and ideas for teaching phonics, as well as presenting devices for recall of irregularly spelled words and meanings of homonyms, improvement of oral reading, and so on.

Goins says: "Numerous comparative investigations of children taught by different methods have shown that any one of the specialized methods has both advantages and limitations; the whole word approach stresses meaning which is the desired end of reading instructions, whereas the phonetic approach develops more accurate word recognition. Today, the evidence of both educational and psychological studies indicates the best results are obtained by stressing both meaning and word recognition from the beginning."[2]

MUSCULAR MOVEMENTS OCCURRING DURING SILENT READING

Sometimes there is concern because young children exhibit lip movements when reading or sounding words. Teachers may feel that this habit slows up reading. It may if carried to extremes, yet much of the fear is unfounded. Mumblings a child uses in trying to decode words do not carry over as much as we think. The child is involved in a mechanical process. This process *must be* mechanical until he or she gains enough power to no longer need those movements and can read smoothly. Many children are unable to develop good eye-voice span in early stages of reading and cannot figure out words before saying them. Frequent admonitions of "Don't move your lips when you read silently" merely create frustration and may impede the child's already laborious attempts to read. It is probably best *not* to eliminate a crutch the child may require, but to substitute help that will eventually supplant the crutch and give the child substantial tools with which to work. Lip movements are usually employed when a child is trying to blend the elements heard and seen to form a whole word.

EFFECTIVE PHONICS

Phonics takes many different forms. Too often in the past, methods of instruction have been offered with no underlying reasons for using them. Research has been scanty and vague. Today's studies show that children given early alphabet and phonics training seem to have greater confidence and ability to help themselves, whereas children taught by only a "look-say" method may become confused when asked to attack an unknown word. More and more teachers are taking an interest in phonics taught by a language-experience approach with coordinated sense training.

THE ORAL-READING PROCESS

Children need to understand something about language structure—its pitches, stresses, and pauses—which are part of a sound system that helps

---

[2]Jean Turner Goins, "Visual and Auditory Perception in Reading," *The Reading Teacher*, October 1959, p. 9.

to convey meaning. Children can learn only by ear the role that variety in the use of tone, loudness, and pause (juncture) can play in conveying meaning. Because oral reading is a means of thought sharing and because a great percentage of time in first grade is devoted to reading aloud, what better opportunity can a teacher have for helping children to read with the expression and proper phrasing necessary to give meaning to context?

Silent reading's importance cannot be minimized; however, it would indeed be folly not to make full use of the primary skills of listening and speech, particularly in initial stages of the reading process. Speech and reading are intimately related, for reading is a form of language expression. Whether we are dealing with forming, receiving, or transmitting language, speech and listening must be established. Many highly coordinated functions and abilities are necessary for reading aloud. First, children must *visualize* a word, *understand* its meaning, and *recall* it before they can read it orally. Second, they must *pronounce* the word understandably and *read* rhythmically. They must move their eyes ahead constantly to grasp the next grouping of words before uttering them. Third, they must "feel" what they are reading and have a desire to communicate to listeners. Furthermore, they must consciously *hear* the words so the ears will get feedback of what is happening.

The ability to read orally is difficult for some children. They constantly think of listeners who approve or disapprove of their performances. If a child is unsure, oral reading will become a chore and a painful experience. John C. Manning says we should encourage "echoic reading," in which the pupil reads the material while listening to the teacher (model) read the same material. Afterward, the pupil reads it independently. Manning says, "This method assists the child in word recognition, develops habits of pupil attention, reduces habits of word-by-word reading, and encourages the use of context cues. Such practices of reading with the teacher helps develop a natural language manner, builds pupil confidence, and general performance."[3]

GENERAL SUGGESTIONS TO IMPROVE ORAL READING

So children will be able to read with variety in speed, loudness, and emphasis and so they will attain interest and confidence in reading, these suggestions are offered.

---

[3]John C. Manning, "Reading-Echoic—An Effective Technique," *Instructor*, November 1971, p. 65. Reprinted from *Instructor*, November 1971. Copyright 1971 by The Instructor Publications, Inc. Used by permission.

○ Ask all children to read a short poem or wall story in unison.

○ Ask a confident child to read a story, and encourage class comment on the expression used: "She sounded as if she were talking and not reading." "I enjoyed listening."

○ Parents or aides can give added time to children's oral reading. They may say, "Let your eyes be brooms and sweep through the words. Start at the left. Tell me if there is a word you do not know. Then you can read the whole sentence without letting any words bother or stop you."

○ Ask the children to clap the rhythm of a memorized poem or sentence.

○ A puppet may do the reading.

○ Omit markers as soon as possible since they are considered crutches.

○ Provide word analysis so children can work out words before reading them aloud.

○ Have a quiet-reading section where children can choose a book and read orally to a selected listener.

○ Use a tape recorder so children may hear themselves read in unison. Be sure that the insecure child *volunteers* for practice.

○ Ask pupils to read along with you so fluency and expression can be improved.

PLANNING A PHONICS PROGRAM

Phonics, to be most effective, should be taught consistently and included within the reading program.

○ *There should be a plan.* Beginning phonics should start with the least complicated concept; gradually add more and more details for children to hear, say, see, and write. The program should introduce perceptual patterns slowly and carefully, integrating them with reading, so meaning is related to the patterns. Step-by-step progression is advised, with frequent review of concepts.

○ *All communication skills should be practiced.* Children need a solid backlog of auditory and verbal experiences previous to and during their kindergarten years, before being introduced to any system demanding visual acuity.

○ *Writing whole words, phrases, and sentences* should definitely be part of any phonics program, not limiting itself merely to circling and underlining of words.

○ *Speech sounds should be pronounced accurately.*

○ *Attention should be paid to recognizing and writing letter forms.*

○ *Too many nonsense syllables, words, or rhymes should be avoided.* "The cat sat on the mat, and that was that" will delight children, but this practice may have little lasting value. Decoding through this medium has no deleterious effect, and children can pick up generalizations; but in presenting nonsense one must be sure it is balanced with stories children can understand, evaluate, and appreciate and to which they can react emotionally.

○ *Key words should be chosen carefully.* They should be easily pictured nouns. Since short vowels usually are taught first, monosyllabic words are chosen if possible. An exception may be *zebra* for *z* or *umbrella* for short *u*.

Plans for Presenting Letter Forms

Teach four consonants at a time until they have been mastered. Such letters as *t* and *f*, and *b* and *d* may be taught together. One must be sure that *t* is familiar before the more difficult form of *f* is presented. Intersperse these consonants with short vowels.

One order for presenting phonics concepts:

Stick letters: T-t, F-f, L-l, H-h, I-i
Stick-curved letters: B-b, D-d, P-p, G-g, R-r, E-e, a
Stick-slant letters: N-n, M-m, W-w, Y-y, Z-z, A
Curved letters: C-c, S-s, Q-q, O-o, U-u
Tail letters: J-j, q, g, y, p

The easier-to-write letters are taught first.

RECALLING REBEL WORDS— 2, 3, 4

These rhymes and devices, developed to help recall rebel words, can be put on wall charts.

THERE–WHERE

There, where, there, where:
Th is the first part of *there;*
Wh is the first part of *where.*
Where is my ball?
It is *there.*

There and *where* can be differentiated by writing both words on the board alternately and placing markers under the *th* and the *wh*.

SAW–WAS

I *was* there and I *saw* you.
The first letters you must sound
So you won't turn the words around.
I *was* there and I *saw* you.

Write both *saw* and *was* on the board. Use an arrow pointing to *s* and *w*.

HOUSE–HORSE

House, horse, house, horse:
Look at the chimney in the house.
[Call attention to *u* and draw a
   column of smoke coming out.]
Look at the saddle on the horse.
[Circle the *r*.]
House, horse, house, horse;
They are not the same, of course.
[You may draw a stick figure sit-
   ting on the *r*.]

PAID–SAID

Paid, said: I said, "Look!
I paid a dollar
For my picture book."
Paid rhymes with *maid* and *raid*.
Said has a short *e* sound.
Said is a rebel word
Where no long *a* is found
And where short *e* is heard
But is not found.

WHO–HOW

Who are you? *How* are you?
Who rhymes with *to*.
How rhymes with *cow*.
Who and *how* are not the same
Look left before you say each name.

Use the three letters on the flannel board and ask the children to re-arrange the letters to form each word.

OUR–OUT

Our, out, our, out:
Our rhymes with *sour*
Out rhymes with *shout*.
R is at the end of *our*,
And *t* is at the end of *out*.

HUNT–HURT

Hunt, hurt, hunt, hurt:
Hunt has *un* as in *fun*
Hurt has *ur* as in *fur*.
Hurt and fur, hunt and fun.

Prolong the *n* when you say *hunt*. Prolong the *r* when you say *hurt*.

ONE

How can we remember to spell
O-n-e and do it well?
Make your mouth round like an *o;*
Make an *n* sound, you will know.
O-n ("oh-nnn"). Did you say *one*?
That was fun!

BUY–BY

By and *buy*, let us try
To spell each one by and by.
I went *by* your *house* and rode my *horse*.
By rhymes with *fly* and *my*.

The *u* in *buy* is a little pocket in which to put your money when you go to the store.

FELT–LEFT

Felt, left, felt, left:
Left begins like *leaf*.
It has short *e* and begins with *l*.
Felt has short *e* too.
And begins with *f*. Can't you tell?

106

Use the four letters on the flannel board or on cards and ask the children to rearrange the letters to form each word. Children may also hold the letters in their hands.

DOES–GOES

> Tom *goes* to school,
> And *goes* begins with *g*.
> *Does* is a rebel word,
> And it begins with *d*.

EVER–VERY

> Very, very, ever, ever:
> *Ever* always rhymes with *never*.
> *Ever* starts with the short vowel *e*,
> While *very* starts with the letter *v*.

LOOK-ALIKES—2, 3, 4

Learning to read and spell words that look almost alike is not easy. A photographic memory process must be used, so these steps may be helpful for children to practice:

1. Pronounce the word.
2. Look at each letter separately from left to right.
3. Try to compare the word to a known one.
4. Close eyes and try to see it.
5. Try to write it.
6. Tell how you remember a particular word.

TEACHING KEY WORDS

WRITE A KEY WORD—1, 2, 3

Write a key word containing a short vowel on the board. Ask a volunteer to erase the first letter and substitute another to make a new word.

BIRTHDAY STORY—1, 2, 3

Ask the children to write all the names of gifts that twins, Betty and Bobby, received for their birthday. Each word must begin with a different letter. The toys may be a stuffed *zebra*, a doll *bed*, a pet *cat* and *duck*, a *fish* in a *bowl*, *gum*, *hats*, *kite*, and so on.

REMEMBERING A KEY WORD—2, 3, 4

Write a row of short-vowel key words across the board. The children cover their eyes. Erase one of the words. The children open their eyes and tell which word was erased.

MATCH THE WORDS—1

Write key words in large letters on strips of construction paper. Place them along the chalk rail. Write the same words on small cards in smaller letters. Ask individual children to match the words.

KEY WORDS IN STORY FORM—2, 3, 4

Duplicate the following poem, which contains nouns that begin with single consonants and short vowels. Do not underline the words. The children read the poem in unison with you. Say: "In this poem you will see the names of many things. The names begin with letter sounds from *a* to *z*. Which name begins with the short *a* vowel? [*apple*] With *b*? [*bed*] With *c*? [*cat*] [And so on.] I will write the names in alphabetical order on the board as you find them. You may then underline them on your copy of the poem. Some words will be underlined twice." The children may dramatize the poem and choose roles to play.

Cat hurt and went to *bed*.
Duck felt bad and said,
I'll take some *fish* for *Cat* to eat.
A *fish* for *Cat* is quite a treat.

Elf heard that *Cat* was sick.
He hurried. He was quick!
"I'll share my pointed *hat* with you,"
He said, "Here's *gum* for you to chew."

Then came the *octopus*.
She came without a fuss.
Her eight long arms were quite a sight.
She brought a *lamp* to give *cat* light.

Pig brought an *apple* red
For *Cat* to eat in *bed*.
Pig said, "Here is a *kite* to fly,
Soon you can fly it in the sky."

Queen came with *jam* and bread
For *Cat* who was in *bed*.
She said, "Here is a *top* of tin,
Here is a *yo-yo* you can spin!"

Rat brought a *nut* to eat.
He left it in the street.
He said, "*Cats* don't like *rats*, you know,
So in my *van* I'll have to go."

The *zebra* said, "This *wig*
Is yours. It's not for *Pig*.
This *box* [x] of candy will be fun.
This *umbrella* is for *sun*.

An *igloo* picture here I drew,
So now I'll trot back to the zoo!"
Cat said, "I don't hurt any more.
I'll use a *mop* to clean the floor.
I am tip-tip! I feel just fine.
I'm glad these friends are friends of mine."

CONSONANTS

THE LOST WORD—2, 3, 4

Teacher: "My word is lost. It is in this room and it begins with *w*."
Individual children may guess *window* or *wall*. The pupil who identifies
the word correctly becomes the leader and thinks of another lost word.
After a word is discovered, a pupil writes it on the board. Encourage
children to ask for help when needed.

DOUBLE CONSONANTS—2, 3, 4

Write these double consonants on the board and ask the children to think
of words that might contain them:

gg   ss   ff   ll   tt   dd   pp   nn   zz   mm

Write the words in parentheses on the board. Tell the pupils that some
double letters will occur in the middle of a word and some will be at the
end. Ask some questions, and invite children to tell which double letters
the answer might contain.

What do we eat for breakfast? It has a shell.   (egg)

You drink from it.   (glass)

What is at the bottom of a sleeve?   (cuff)

What do you wear when you catch a baseball?   (mitt)

What sound does a bee make?   (buzz)

What grows on a tree, has a stem, and sometimes is red or yellow? It is good to eat.   (apple)

You put it on a horse.   (saddle)

We find it at the beach.   (shell)

When we say "two plus two," what do we do?   (add)

It is like jam. You spread it on bread.   (jelly)

It goes with a nail.   (hammer)

It is a cent.   (penny)

You wear it on your foot.   (slipper)

SILENT LETTERS—2, 3, 4

k   b   l   g   w

Duplicate a page of verses minus the silent letter. The pupils write the correct silent letter to complete the word. They may take turns reading the verses.

Yum, yum, yum!
There is jam on my thum___ .

My paper is white.
A poem I will ___rite.

I went to the zoo
And I saw a ___nu.

I call him Sam.
He is my pet lam___ .

Oh, dear me!
I hurt my ___nee.

I cut a board in ha___f.
A young cow is a ca___f.

A stop si___n is red.
"Stop!" I said.

It is not a cat or bat.
It is a tiny ___nat.

If I bend my ___rist,
I can make a fist.

Will you wa___k with me?
Will you ta___k with me?

INITIAL, MEDIAL, FINAL—3, 4

The children sit in a circle. Name an alphabet letter, such as *s*. Then name a word. If the *s* sound is at the beginning (*Sam*) the children say the word and touch their heads. If *s* is at the end (*bus*), they touch their feet. If *s* is in the middle (*basket*), they touch their "tummies."

SOFT c—3, 4

C has the s sound when it is followed by i or e. Duplicate this exercise. Ask pupils to pronounce the words with soft c and supply the last word in each sentence. You may use echoic reading, in which pupils and teachers read simultaneously, or the children may repeat the sentences after you.

Which one would you eat for breakfast?   (cereal)
Which one is the top of a room?   (celing)
Which one is a round shape?   (circle)
Which one means "the middle"?   (center)
Which one has many legs?   (centipede)

Encourage pupils to look up in their dictionaries words that begin with soft c and divide them into syllables, or parts of words, as in cen-ti-pede.

SOFT c AT THE BEGINNING, END, OR IN THE MIDDLE—3, 4

Ask pupils to work out these words and use them in sentences:

tricycle	sauce	fireplace	centimeter
twice	license	center	spaceship
bicycle	bracelet	iceberg	circular

THE SOFT g SOUND—3, 4

Duplicate the following words and ask the pupils to underline each g that has the sound of j. They also tell the number of syllables in each word.

gentle	sponge	cage	giant
badger	orange	baggage	pigeon
pledge	engine	angel	gingerbread
geography	giraffe	hedge	huge

Ask these questions. Pupils underline the correct answers from the preceding list of words.

Which one is a tall animal? A huge man? Kind? A book of maps?
A cake? An animal? A fruit? Part of a car? A place for a lion?
A bird? A suitcase? A plant? Part of a Christmas tree?
Which one comes from the ocean?
Which one means big? Another word for a promise?

Ask pupils to tell in which part of the word they heard soft *g:* first, middle, or end.

CONSONANT DIGRAPHS

DIGRAPH BASEBALL—3, 4

Draw a baseball diamond shape on the board and write *sh, ch, th,* and *wh* at each angle or corner. If a child can name a word beginning with each digraph, he or she has made a home run. Write their contributions on the board.

Ch-sh WALL CHART—3, 4

On a sheet of heavy tagboard, write *ch* words on one side and *sh* words on the other. Attach the chart to a wire coat hanger and use binder rings so it can be hung on the wall.

These words can help the Spanish-speaking child who confuses the two sounds:

chair	shoe	chore
chew	shop	ship
chop	chip	sheep
share	cheap	shore

Another chart can be made for voiceless *th* words for which *s* or *f* sounds may be substituted or misarticulated.

thumb	sum (or some)	thick	sick
three	free	thank	sank
think	sink	throw	fro

THE MERRY-GO-ROUND—2, 3, 4

The two words *shall* and *choose* in the following poem will provide practice for the *sh* and *ch* sounds. Ask the children to listen as you read it.

Listen to the circus sound
Of the music on the merry-go-round.
Shall I *choose* a horse of white,
And hold the reins with all my might?
Shall I choose a horse of brown

That proudly paces up and down?
Shall I choose a horse of black
With shiny blanket on its back?

Ask individuals which horse they would *choose*. Write the poem on a wall chart for third and fourth graders to read.

USING THE CONSONANT DIGRAPH *ch* IN CONVERSATION—1, 2, 3, 4

Provide a box of articles whose names contain the digraph *ch*. They may be wrapped *cheese*, a piece of *chalk*, wrapped *chocolate*, a *chain*, a little bag of *cherries*, a book of *matches* closed, and a doll *chair*.

Elicit complete sentences as follows.

Say: *Choose* something.   Child: I will *choose* a _____.
Say: Write your name with *chalk*.   Child: I will write my name with *chalk*.
Sit in a *chair*.   Child: I will sit in a *chair*.
Point to your *chest* and *chin*. [Response]
Pretend to eat *chocolate*. [Response.]
Point to your left *cheek*. [Response.]
What are *cherries* for? [Response.]
Where would you see a *chimpanzee*? [Response.]

WITCH WANDA—2, 3, 4

When you finish reading the story, ask children to relate as many events as they can. Each statement must have a word with *ch* at the beginning or at the end. You may duplicate the story, omitting italicized words. Give each child a copy, and ask the class to underline all the words that have the *ch* sound.

Witch Wanda took out her *watch*. She *chuckled*. It was time for Halloween. She *chose* a black cat to ride on her broomstick. His name was *Charcoal*.

Witch Wanda scrubbed the *porch* and dusted the *chairs*. Then she decided to have *lunch*. She went out to *chop* wood and make a fire. The smoke poured up the *chimney*. She took out her best *china* cups and saucers. She set the table for *lunch*. When it was ready, she had *cherry* tarts, lamb *chops*, *chop* suey, *peach* pie, a *cheese sandwich*, fried *chicken*, clam *chowder*, *chili*, and *poached* eggs.

After *lunch*, she sat down and played a game of *checkers*.

113

At last night came, so Witch Wanda got on her broom with *Charcoal* and off they went to the moon.

The children may draw pictures of the story and back them for the flannel board. They can retell the story, using these pictures and trying to recall words that have the *ch* sound.

Sh MAKES JUST ONE SOUND—2, 3, 4

S and *h* make just one sound
You hear in *shoe* and *shell*.
But you can hear it at the end
Of *dish* and *fish* as well!

USING THE *sh* CONSONANT DIGRAPH IN CONVERSATION—3, 4

Articles for a consonant digraph box containing the *sh* sound are a small bottle of *shampoo*, a toy *shovel*, a *shirt*, a *dish*, a *brush*, a *flashlight*, a *shell*, a *shawl*, and a *shoe*. Ask for complete sentences as you say:

Show me your right *shoe*. Child: I will *show* you my right *shoe*. [Change to left.]
Shine your *shoe*. Child: I will *shine* my *shoe*.
Give me a bottle of *shampoo*. [Response.]
Shake your arm. [Response.]
What is *sharp?* [Response.]
Show me a *shell*. [Response.]
Who wears a *shawl?* [Response.]
Who is wearing a *shirt?* [Response.]
What would you do with a *shovel?* [Response.]
Is a cup a *dish?* [Response.]
Is a *sheep* an animal? [Response.]

RIDDLES—1, 2, 3

Children supply the word that answers each riddle, which must begin with *sh*.

It rhymes with tack. It is an old house. It is a _____ . (shack)
It rhymes with keep. It is a woolly animal. It is a _____ . (sheep)
It rhymes with dirt. You wear it. It is a _____ . (shirt)
It rhymes with bell. It is at the beach. It is a _____ . (shell)

LASSO THE WORDS—2, 3, 4

Draw a large circle representing a lasso on the board. Inside the circle, write words beginning with voiced *th:*

the	that	this	they	these
them	those	though	then	there

This exercise will help the child with substandard speech. The pupils say this verse with you and then individuals pronounce the words:

Lasso these sight words!
Don't let them get away,
Because you will use them
Almost every day.

MAKE A STORY FOR THE *wh* DIGRAPH—2, 3, 4

Mount large magazine pictures that have good story content. Below each picture, write these words: *What? Where? When? Why?* and *Who?* Explain that *who* begins with the sound of *h* and not the sound of *wh*.

Have the children make short stories. Here is an example:

Who? Fido.
What happened? Fido barked.
Where? Fido barked outside my window.
When? Fido barked last night.
Why? Fido barked at a stray cat.

THE *ng* CONSONANT DIGRAPH

Duplicate this exercise. Ask the pupils to complete each word with *ng* and write sentences containing the words.

ri____	wi____	ba____	lo____
hu____	si____	so____	go____

BELLS—2, 3, 4

This poem, which contains many words with the *ng* consonant digraph, can be put on a wall chart. It can be used for choral speaking as well as for locating words with the consonant digraph. Ask the children to listen for the *ng* sound.

A long bell, a strong bell,
Ding, dong, ding!
A song bell, a wrong bell,
Ping, pong, ping!

The songs were sung and bells were rung
In winter and in spring.
I walked along and sang a song
As happy as a king.

A long bell, a strong bell,
Ding, dong, ding!
A song bell, a wrong bell,
Ping, pong, ping!

ADDING *ing* TO WORDS—2, 3, 4

Children who substitute *n* for *ng*, as in *singin'* for *singing*, will benefit from practice with the *ing* suffix. This exercise can be duplicated or pupils may supply the rhyming word orally.

Mules are kicking.
Clocks are _____ . (ticking)

Roosters are crowing.
Plants are _____ . (growing)

Eggs are frying.
Birds are _____ . (flying)

Meat is roasting.
Bread is _____ . (toasting)

If a word ends with *e*, the *e* is dropped before *ing* is added:

Leaves are for raking.
Cakes are for _____ . (baking)

Sometimes we go biking.
Or else we go _____ . (hiking)

WORDS WITH *nk*—2, 3, 4

Sometimes *n* has the sound of *ng*. Duplicate this exercise for the class to complete.

We keep some junk
Inside an old _____ . (trunk)

The water was drunk
By a black and white _____ . (skunk)

My mother does not think
A baby should write with _____ . (ink)

Hank and Frank
Have a big piggy _____. (bank)

The horses drank
From an old tin _____ . (tank)

I like to drink
Lemonade that is _____ . (pink)

THE SEPARATE SOUNDS OF *n*
AND *g*—3, 4

Sometimes *n* and *g* have separate sounds. The *n* has the sound of *ng*. The *g* sounds like *g* in *goat*. Here are examples that are syllabicated:

1. tri-an-gle 2. fin-ger 3. hun-gry
4. an-gry 5. lan-guage 6. rec-tan-gle

Duplicate the following exercise. Ask the children to write the numeral of the meaning of each word or words in the space provided.

A shape with three sides ____
A shape with four sides ____
What we speak ____
Mad ____
On your hand ____
Needing food ____

THE *ph* AND *gh* CONSONANT
DIGRAPHS—4 (Advanced)

These words may be worked out by more advanced pupils. They should use their dictionaries, write each word, and divide it into syllables; then use the words in oral or written sentences. Tell the pupils that both digraphs have the *f* sound.

ph: geography, nephew, photograph, elephant, Philadelphia
gh: laugh, tough, trough, enough

CONSONANT BLENDS

GROWLY BEAR—1, 2, 3, 4

On brown construction paper draw a large bear raised on its haunches. Around the front paws cut slits in which word cards can be inserted. Paste the figure to a sheet of tagboard and leave the paws free. Make word cards using words that begin with the *r* blends and contain long or short vowels. Here are some suggestions:

crab   grapes   tree   bride   prize   frame   drum

L blends, such as the following, could also be used.

globe   plane   flag   clock   block   slacks

Children may find in their readers other words beginning with these blends. Encourage them to make word cards for the bear.

WHISPERING WORDS—3, 4

Write on the board a list of words containing initial consonant blends. Call a child's name and whisper. "Is the word _____ on the board?" The child must, of course, recognize the word and name it.

TWINS AND TRACKS, BLENDS
FOR WALL CHARTS—3, 4

The pupils read the following duplicated rhymes with you orally and select words with blends.

Twin children, twin skates,	Tracks are made by tires
Twin frogs that are mates.	On tractors, cars, and trucks.
Twin mittens, twelve in all;	Tracks are made by twins and
Twenty pictures on the wall.	Trailers, bikes, and ducks.

THE *s* CONSONANT BLENDS—3, 4

Note that all noun words beginning with consonant blends contain long or short vowels; however, since the children should realize that there are other vowel sounds, encourage them to look for words with *s* blends in their readers. These words with blends can be written on separate slips of paper for the children to read orally and use in sentences. (Note that three words begin with three-letter blends, *str, scr, spr.*)

stone	swine
snake	scream
scale	skate
spot	street
smoke	squid
sled	spring

These couplets can be duplicated or used orally. Children say or write the last word in the second line.

My dog found a bone.
It was under a ＿＿＿＿＿ . (stone)

We like to swing
In summer or ＿＿＿＿＿ . (spring)

I cannot be seen
Behind a ＿＿＿＿＿ . (screen)

I went to the beach. Yes, I did.
I picked up seashells and a ＿＿＿＿＿ . (squid)

The folks awoke
And smelled some ＿＿＿＿＿ . (smoke)

Alice said
That she likes her new ＿＿＿＿＿ . (sled)

I hear running feet
Go down the ＿＿＿＿＿ . (street)

Out by the lake,
We saw a large ＿＿＿＿＿ . (snake)

I made a dot,
And it left a big ＿＿＿＿＿ . (spot)

A pig is my pet and it is mine.
A pig will always be a ＿＿＿＿＿ . (swine).

My friend Dale
Was weighed on a ＿＿＿＿＿ . (scale)

My pal Kate
Likes to ＿＿＿＿＿ . (skate)

FINAL CONSONANT BLENDS—3, 4

The pupils supply the last word in the last line of each of these couplets either in writing or orally. Write these blends on the board:

nd   nt   mp   st   rm   rn   rk   rt

The scouts all went
To sleep in a _____ . (tent)

I hold some sand
Inside my _____ . (hand)

We need some yarn
For the socks we _____ . (darn)

Bill got some dirt
On his new _____. (shirt)

Frank uses his arm
To pitch hay on the _____ . (farm)

Out in the park,
We heard a dog _____ . (bark)

A hen likes to rest
Inside her warm _____ . (nest)

A rabbit can jump
Over a _____ . (stump)

Ask pupils to find words in their readers that end with blends.

SHORT VOWELS

Short vowels usually are taught first in a phonics program. It would therefore seem logical to devise a sequence in teaching them so that children will begin developing "phonics power." The rationale for presenting short vowels first is that children appear to have more difficulty hearing and pronouncing them than other vowel sounds. Short vowels have more than one pronunciation. Short *e* (*pen*) and short *i* (*pig*) are particularly difficult to hear accurately in isolation, for they cannot be prolonged as easily as short *a*, *o*, and *u*.

Children can visualize a three-letter short-vowel word as a whole because of the one vowel. They can substitute an initial or final consonant and create a new word. Long-vowel words (*cake, rope, cute, Pete, rice*) often contain two vowels, one of them silent, and very young children are often not ready for generalizations or rules. By blending the initial consonant and its succeeding short vowel, we have a consonant–short vowel blend (*ca, be, so*). Thus, when pronouncing *ca-t*, the child is saying the word as it is *spoken.*

SHORT *a* AND SHORT *o*—2, 3

Ask the children to open the mouth widely when they hear you say a word with short *a* and point to the lips when you say a word with short *o*. Note that we open the mouth widely for short *o*, too. They write the word, then substitute a short vowel to make a new word.

hat	fan	man	cot	nob
Tom	cap	John	hot	Jack
top	ran	tap	mop	bag

Ask individual children to pronounce a word and use it in a sentence. Write their sentences on the board.

Note: Do not include words ending with *og* since some of them have the sound of *aw*. For first graders use this as an auditory exercise.

SHORT *i* AND SHORT *u*—2, 3

Ask the children to hold up a forefinger when they hear a word with short *i* and make a u shape with thumb and forefinger when they hear a word with short *u*. They write each word from dictation and substitute a short vowel to make a new word.

fun	tub	wig	bill	pig
fish	pin	run	duck	nut
bus	big	cup	gum	dip

Note: For first graders, use this as an auditory exercise.

SHORT *o* AND SHORT *e*—2, 3

Ask the children to make a circle with the forefingers when you say a word with short *o* and smile when you say a word with short *e*. Write the words on the board.

hen	pot	red	not	mop
get	bell	box	net	Ted
pen	cot	bed	fox	jet

Then say the consonant–short vowel blend (e.g., *mo* or *re*) only and invite children to point to the word, say it, and make a sentence. They may substitute another short vowel to make a new word.

RHYMES TO COMPLETE—1, 2, 3

Say these rhymes for the children to complete aloud. Duplicate for second and third graders to write the rhyming words.

My pup's name is Tag
See his tail _____ . (wag)

I do not want ham.
I want grape _____ . (jam)

My little bed
Is blue and _____ . (red)

My pet hen
Is in a _____ . (pen)

I think I will
Go up the _____ . (hill)

There is a rock
Inside my _____ . (sock)

I like to hop
And play with my _____ . (top)

The little red bug
Is on my _____ . (rug)

Yum, yum, yum,
Get some _____ . (gum)

Bus, bus,
Come and take _____ . (us)

WORD-STRIP CUTTING—2, 3, 4

On a long strip of paper 6 inches wide, write words with short vowels 2 inches apart. If a child can say the word, she or he may cut it off the strip. This same device may be used for initial consonants, long vowels, or any other phonics concept.

LITTLE WORDS IN BIG WORDS—2, 3, 4

Tell the children that *and* can be part of two- and three-syllable words. Duplicate these verses and ask the children to underline the *and* part of the words.

A sandwich is never
Made of sand.
A bandage never
Plays in the band.

A lifeguard sits
Up in a stand.
People lie there
In the sand.

A candle makes
A dandy light.
It is so handy
In the night.

A handbag holds
A lot of things
Like candy,
Rubber bands, and rings.

WHEN o HAS THE SHORT-u SOUND— 3, 4

Duplicate this list of words. The pupils write the numeral that stands for the definition next to each phrase. Then they read the phrases and write the actual word instead of the numeral on the line provided. (Be sure the line is long enough for the missing word.)

1. honey	5. monkey	9. mother
2. dozen	6. sponge	10. money
3. tongue	7. stomach	11. Monday
4. glove	8. brother	12. oven

A long-tailed animal _____ (monkey)
Twelve of something _____ (dozen)
For a hand _____ (glove)
Where food goes _____ (stomach)
A woman _____ (mother)
Day of the week _____ (Monday)
Pennies _____ (money)
Made by bees _____ (honey)
In your mouth _____ (tongue)
A man _____ (brother)
Soaks up water _____ (sponge)
Part of a stove _____ (oven)

LONG VOWELS

THE ea VOWEL DIGRAPH—2, 3, 4

This generalization may be written on a chart or duplicated. Read it and discuss the rule as exemplified in the rhyme.

Leaf, meat, seal, and *bean.*

When *e* and *a* are side by side,
The vowel *a* says, "I will hide,
And let my friend *e* say its name;
But I will stay here just the same."

Ask the pupils to write the four words. Then have them cross out the silent *a* and place a macron over the long *e*.

LONG *e* AT THE END—2, 3, 4

He, me, be, we, and *she*
Are little words, you will agree.
But only one *e* you will find.
The other *e* was left behind.

Use in the same way as the *ea* vowel digraph.

LONG *i* WITH LAZY *e*—2, 3, 4

Kite, five, pine, dime, and *tire.*

In these five words, long *i* is found,
But lazy *e* makes not a sound.

Use in the same way as the *ea* vowel digraph.

LONG *a* WITH LAZY *e*—2, 3, 4

Rake, bake, cake, make, and *fade.*

Vowels *a* and *e* are both in sight.
Vowel *a* is left and *e* is right.

Use in the same way as the *ea* vowel digraph.

THE *oa* VOWEL DIGRAPH—2, 3, 4

Goat, boat, Joan, loan, and *coal.*

Round *o* her letter name will keep,
While lazy *a* goes fast asleep.

Use in the same way as the *ea* vowel digraph.

LONG *u* WITH SILENT *E*—2, 3, 4

Mule, cube, cute, fuse, and *hue.*

When we say *mule,* we use long *u,*
But *e* is still and lazy too.

Use in the same way as the *ea* vowel digraph.

CONTRASTING LONG- AND
SHORT-VOWEL WORDS—2, 3, 4

Write short-vowel words on short strips and long-vowel words on longer strips. The length of the paper or tagboard, together with the length of the word, may help the children understand the concept of long and short in connection with vowels. Suggested pairs are

met–meat	hid–hide	neat–net
can–cane	Tim–time	mat–mate
pin–pine	got–goat	cub–cube
rip–ripe	cut–cute	seat–set

MORE WORDS WITH LONG e—4
(ADVANCED)

Write this rule on a chart or on the board and read it with the class.

An *i* before *e* except after *c*
Is one of our reading clues.
So let us remember how to spell
All of these words we use.

Write these words on the board.

brief	yield	chief
grief	field	niece
shriek	thief	belief

Ask the nine questions and let individual children answer your questions. They point to the correct word on the board and say it. They make complete sentences using the words. The exercise may be duplicated.

What does short mean?
What does yell mean?
Where is wheat grown?
What is a head engineer called?
Do you have an opinion? What is it?
What does sadness mean?
What does "give in" mean?
Who is a person who steals things?
What is your brother or sister's child called?

THE *ight* FAMILY—3, 4

List these words on the board.

Night	Fright	Light	Fight
Sight	might	right	

Underline *ight*. Explain that *g* and *h* are silent and that *ight* sounds like *ite*. Duplicate the poem. Read it aloud with the class. Then ask the children to use one of the *ight* words in a sentence. They underline all *ight* words in the poem.

Night is quiet; night is nice
For sleeping people and little mice.
Fright was fear when I heard a sound.
It was only wind and leaves, I found.
Light is bright for run and play.
Light is part of every day.
Sight belongs to you and me.
There are so many sights to see.
Fight can usually be seen
Between two cats on Halloween.
I listen hard with all my might,
And try to learn my phonics right.

Ow WITH THE SOUND OF LONG *o*—3, 4

List these words on the board and discuss the sound of long *o*.

slow	show	crow	know	throw
flow	row	bow	grow	glow

Duplicate the list of questions. The children write *yes* or *no* after each one.

Can a crow row a boat? _____
Can a toad grow? _____
Can a goat throw a ball? _____
Is an ant slow? _____
Do you know some words? _____
Can a fire glow? _____
Can you see a puppet show? _____
Can water flow? _____

WORDS ENDING IN *old*—3, 4

Old is a word, yet it can be part of a word. List these words on the board for the children to pronounce

old   cold   gold   scold   fold   told   sold   bold

Individual children point to the word that answers your question. They spell the word and use it in a sentence.

What is the opposite of new?
What is the opposite of hot?
What means brave?
What did you do with a story?
What happens to things in a store?
What is a ring made from?
What do you do with your hands?
What would you do if the puppy dug up your flowers?

REBEL WORDS—3, 4

neigh   weigh   sleigh   reindeer

Ei has the sound of long *a*. Duplicate this poem for the children to read orally and select the words with the *ei* combination.

"Neigh" is a sound that a pony makes.
You stand on a scale to weigh.
A sleigh carries Santa pulled by reindeer
With presents for Christmas day.

APOSTROPHE—3, 4 (ADVANCED)

List on a chart the words with apostrophes so the children can refer to them when completing or writing sentences, and duplicate the exercise below. Say: "These apostrophes mean that one or more letters have been left out. What would we say for *It is?* (*It's*) Here are some words with letters left out. See if you can complete the lines with apostrophe words." If necessary, direct the children in the use of capital and lower-case letters.

she's	he'll	we'll	it's
they're	you've	can't	we've
he's	she'll	they'll	you'll
they've	won't	I've	I'll

_____ snowing today. (It's)

Birds are gone. _____ be back next spring. (They'll)

_____ a pilot. She likes the job. (She's)

My father is coming home. _____ be here tonight. (He'll)

If you don't hurry _____ be late. (you'll)

You have a pet. _____ got one too. (I've) _____ a gerbil. (It's)

_____ be your friend. (I'll)

Will you go to the moon? No, I _____ . (won't) Can you go to the moon? No, I _____ . (can't)

Ann and Jim said, "_____ have pink lemonade at the circus." (We'll)

Mary will visit us. _____ be here next week. (She'll)

We have some friends. _____ here from Kansas. (They're)

_____ my brother. (He's)

My friends are not here. _____ not come yet. (They've)

Where is your hat? I bet _____ lost it. (you've)

Do you have a dog? _____ two of them. (We've)

COMPOUND WORDS—3, 4

Explain that compound words contain more than one vowel sound. The vowel denotes the basic unit of a syllable, and words sometimes have one, two, three, or even more syllables. All the compound words in this list contain two syllables and long and short vowels only. Write the words on a chart or duplicate them for follow-up. The children draw a macron over each long vowel and a line under each short vowel. They use the words in sentences.

pigtail	padlock	mailbox	pancake	pickax
necktie	railroad	bedbug	sailboat	hayride
billfold	pinwheel	daylight	beehive	handbag
gumdrop	rainbow	rowboat	cupcake	drumstick
tugboat	cockroach	sunshine	wigwag	snowflake

SYLLABICATION—3, 4

In structural analysis, there is a linkage between syllables and word meanings. Encourage the children to look up the words on this page in their dictionaries to see how many syllables each word contains. They then write the words, divide them into syllables, put in the accent mark, and write the number of syllables.

padlock	taxicab	lollipop	violin
acrobat	pinecone	dustpan	spaceship
bicycle	hippopotamus	handball	fireplace

As an additional exercise the pupils may draw a macron over long vowels and underline all short vowels. Discuss other vowel sounds with them.

HOMONYMS—3, 4

Explain that homonyms are words that sound the same but have different spellings and meanings. Ask the pupils to underline homonyms twice and draw a macron over each long vowel. Duplicate the poems. Duplicate them again and omit the homonyms for the children to fill in.

Made-Maid

A *maid* went to market
Some butter to buy,
And when she came home,
She *made* a peach pie.

Meat-Meet

I will *meet* you at three,
And then we will shop
To buy some fresh *meat*
At the butcher shop.

Beet-Beat

A *beet* is a vegetable,
And so good to eat.
Can you *beat* me racing
Down this long street?

To-Two-Too

Two hats *to* one head are *too*
    many.
Can you draw that picture
    for me?
Two has a silent *w;*
And that is a number, you see.
To means to go to school.
I'll go, *too*, which means *also*.
How cool!

Heel-Heal

I have a big sore on my *heel*.
My shoes were much too tight.
My brother says my *heel* will
    heal.
It may *heal* overnight.

Here-Hear

Here means put the book right
    here.
Please come *here!* Can you *hear?*
Hear means that you have heard
    the sound
That travels to your ear.

Yoke-Yolk

An ox wore a *yoke* around its
    neck
When it pulled a wagon or plow.
A hen lays an egg that has a *yolk*.
She cackles and then takes a bow.

Break-Brake

Be sure the *brake* holds on your
    car,
Or you might not travel very far.
You can get a *"break"* or *break*
    an egg.
But be careful not to *break* your
    leg.

THE SOUND OF LONG *u*—4
(ADVANCED)

When *u* is followed by *e*, often *u* says its alphabet name (as in *cube*). Write these words on the board. Ask the children to name them, use them in sentences, and draw a macron over each long *u*.

mule	cute	cube	use	fuse
refuse	dispute	fumes	excuse	hue

Explain that the *u* is long when it is an accented beginning syllable.

pupil	bugle	beautiful
humorous	usual	cucumber
uniform	fuel	beauty (silent *e* and *a*)

Explain that in an accented second syllable, the *u* may be long.

abuse   perfume   confuse

Rebel words:

you   feud   youth   Hugh

Ask individual children to point to the word on the board or chart that answers your question. They should also answer in a complete statement, such as "The mule has long ears."

What do you say when you sneeze? (Excuse me.)
Which animal has long ears and a loud bray? (mule)
Which word means funny? (humorous)
Which one is a strange bird? (emu)
Which one is a six-sided figure? (cube)
Which one is a dress suit? (uniform)

Children may then supply their own questions. Ask a volunteer to look up information on emus.

OTHER VOWEL SOUNDS

THE SOUND OF LONG *oo*—3, 4

Children can complete these rhymes orally, or you may duplicate them.

I lost my tooth
In a telephone _____ . (booth)

A kangaroo
Lives at the _____ . (zoo)

Blue is cool
Like water in a _____ . (pool)

Don't sail a balloon
Around the _____ . (room)

The chicken brood
Ate all the _____ . (food)

We saw a raccoon
By the light of the _____ . (moon)

WORKING OUT WORDS WITH LONG
oo—3, 4

Duplicate these words and syllabicate them. The pupils will draw a macron over each *oo*. Children will pronounce the words and use them in sentences.

cartoon	toothbrush
toadstool	caboose
fireproof	bathroom
scooter	igloo

WHAT WE SEE AT THE ZOO—3, 4

Use this poem for a wall chart. The children read the poem in unison and discover and pronounce words that have long *oo*. Ask them to add other animals that have the *oo* sound (*hoopsnake, raccoon*).

At the Zoo

A big baboon is in a cage.
There is a cockatoo.
A girl is leading a poodle.
We see these things at the zoo.

There is a hopping kangaroo,
And there is a very large moose.
We see a boy with a red balloon,
But we see no rooster or goose.

131

OTHER LONG *oo* SPELLINGS—3, 4

These words contain the *ou* spelling but the sound of long *oo*. Write them on the board and pronounce them with the class.

group	Louis	route (sometimes pronounced *rowt*)
toucan	you	wound (sometimes pronounced with *ow* sound)
soup	you'd	

Sometimes *ew* also has the sound of long *oo*.

blew	brew	crew	threw	chew
drew	jewel	flew	cashew	stew

Duplicate these sentences for the children to complete using the above words.

The wind _____ . (blew) The ship's _____ (crew) was on the sea. Seagulls _____ (flew) by the ship and its crew. A _____ (crew) member _____ (drew) a picture of the sea and the seagulls. They _____ (threw) spoiled food overboard. The ship's _____ (crew) liked to _____ (chew) gum and eat _____ (cashew) nuts. The cook would _____ (brew) their tea. He had a bright green _____ (jewel) in his ring. At night he like to make meat _____ (stew) for dinner.

SINGLE *u* WITH THE SOUND OF LONG *oo*—3, 4

1. suit	2. fruit	3. juice	4. blue	5. ruby
6. glue	7. tuna	8. June	9. plume	

The children write the numeral of the word or phrase listed below.

Apples _____
For drinking _____
A color _____
Feather _____
Fish _____

A month _____
A kind of paste _____
A stone _____
Clothing _____

SELECTING CORRECT WORDS—3, 4

Write these poems on the board or on a chart, or duplicate them. The children select and write words with *u* that have the sound of long *oo*.

The Flag

We salute the flag,
'Red, white, and blue.
Red means "brave,"
And blue means "true."

Bruce

When Bruce played a flute
In the band last June,
He tried very hard
To keep in tune.

THE SOUND OF SHORT *oo*—3, 4

Duplicate this story, containing words with the sound of short *oo*. The children underline and write all words with the short *oo* sound.

The Collection

Mrs. Darby collects books. The oldest book is *Red Riding Hood*. The best books are about woodpeckers and woodchucks.

Mrs. Darby also collects fishhooks. She has a looking glass and a wooden bench. They are 50 years old. She collects pictures of woolly animals like sheep. She collects pictures of babbling brooks.

Mrs. Darby does not collect cookies. She bakes them and gives them to her friends.

WHEN *u* HAS THE SOUND OF SHORT *oo*—2, 3, 4

Draw an irregularly shaped *bush*. Inside, write these words.

bush	sugar	bushel	push
butcher	pudding	cushion	put

Invite children to "pull a word out of the bush," say it, and use it in a sentence.

DIPHTHONGS

A diphthong ("dif-thong") consists of a movement or glide from one vowel to another. The two elements are said quickly in succession and pronounced smoothly, with no interruption in phonation.

The first vowel is stressed in *ow* and *oy*, and the mouth opening is larger for the first than for the second part of the diphthong.

PRONOUNCING WORDS WITH *OW*—3, 4

Write these words on rectangular tagboard shapes. Invite children to see how many they can say and then drop them into a sack or box labeled *ow*.

cow   owl   growl   allow   howl   now   down   how
gown   bow (also pronounced with long *o* as in *crow*)
scowl   clown   prowl   fowl   shower   flower
coward   Howard   vowel   towel   crown   town

Ask members of the class to complete these duplicated rhymes with words that contain *ow:*

Down came a shower,
And up grew a _____ .   (flower)

Do not write vowels
On bathroom _____ .   (towels)

A queen wears a crown
And a velvet _____ .   (gown)

The big horned owl
Has a very big _____ .   (scowl)

THE *ou* DIPHTHONG—3, 4

Ow and *ou* are twins. Write these words on the board and ask the pupils to pronounce and use them in sentences. Pupils tell which words rhyme.

south   mouth   grouch   pouch
ground   sound   hour   sour

THE *oi* AND *oy* DIPHTHONGS—3, 4
(Advanced)

Ask the pupils to pronounce these words that have the sound of *oi.*

1. coin   2. oil   3. Detroit   4. doily   5. soil
6. point   7. foil   8. toil   9. coil

Duplicate the following words and phrases and direct the children to write the numeral of the correct answer in each blank.

Something for wrapping food _____   A city _____
End of a pencil _____   To work _____
Something a car uses _____   Earth _____
Something to put under a vase _____   A penny _____
To curl up _____

134

Pronounce these words that have the sound of *oy*, and ask individual children to use them in sentences.

boy   toy   enjoy   oyster   destroy

READING COMPREHENSION—3, 4

The pupils write *yes* or *no* in answer to these duplicated questions:

Is a boy a person? _____
Is an oyster good to eat? _____
If you enjoy something, does that mean you like it? _____
Is a school bus a toy? _____
Does *destroy* mean to build something? _____

VOWELS MODIFIED BY *r*

These vowels *a*, *e*, *i*, *o*, and *u* may be modified by the consonant *r*. There are regional differences in pronunciation. The following exercises will help the children to understand the influence of *r* on the vowel that it follows.

VOWEL *i* MODIFIED BY *r*—4

These words may be written on flash cards or on the board and pronounced by the class. Ask the pupils to copy the words and underline *ir*.

sir	whir	third	thirst
whirl	chirp	first	birthday
stir	bird	girl	dirt
twirl	skirt	birch	stirrups

SENTENCES CONTAINING WORDS
WITH *ir*—3, 4

Write these sentences on the board. Ask individual children to select and underline words that contain *ir*. Tell them that some of the words will have two syllables.

Kirk is a man.
My friend has a birthday.
The shirt is dirty.
Thirteen boys are at camp.
A squirrel lives in a tree.

Clowns are in a circus.
You say "sir" to a man.
A bird can be thirsty.
A saddle has stirrups.
A bird chirps.

WORDS WITH *ur*—3, 4

These words can be written on the board, pronounced, and used in sentences. Ask children to write a sentence using at least one word.

cur	purse	spurs	curve
burst	nurse	turtle	jury
surf	purr	Thursday	burn
curls	turnip	hurt	hurry
fur	purple	curb	burden
turn	church	turkey	spurn

WORDS WITH *er*—3, 4

The children look up these words in their dictionaries. They may divide the words into syllables and use them in written sentences or pronounce them orally and tell their meanings. *Note:* Explain that the word *handkerchief* has a silent *d* and is pronounced "hang-ker-chif" (short *i*).

were	germ	sherbet
jerk	handkerchief	verse
perfume	fern	nerve
perch	Bert	deserve
clerk	termite	merchant
iceberg	stern	serve
verb	Verna	hermit

USING WORDS WITH *ur*—3, 4

Ask the children to pronounce these words that have the sound of *ur*.

1. burst	2. nurse	3. gurgle	4. purr
5. turn	6. hurt	7. curl	8. burn

Duplicate the following incomplete sentences. The pupils write the numeral of the word that completes each sentence.

Wood will _____ .
Balloons will _____ .
The person is a _____ .
Hair will _____ .

Water will _____ .
Wheels will _____ .
Cats will _____ .
Cuts can _____ .

Rebel word: *bury* ("berry").

WORDS WITH *ur* AND THE SOUND OF
SHORT *oo*—4 (Advanced)

curious	mural	adventure	Europe
cure	furious	pure	secure

Ask the pupils to look up these words in the dictionary to verify the pronunciation of short *oo*.

Ear WITH THE SOUND OF *er*—3, 4

Duplicate these words. Explain that *a* is silent. Ask the children to use each word in a sentence.

earth   learn   heard   search   pearl   Earl

Rebel word: *heart*.

Or WITH THE SOUND OF *er*—3, 4

These words should be learned by sight. Ask children to use them in sentences.

worry   worm   word   work   world   worse

Er WITH THE SOUND OF *ear*—3, 4

Suggest that the pupils look up these words in the dictionary, divide them into syllables, and use them in sentences.

cereal	mysterious	superior	serious
cashier	sphere	severe	

Duplicate the following words and phrases and ask the children to write the correct defining word in each blank.

Strange _____
Breakfast food _____
One who handles money _____
Not funny _____
Better _____
A globe _____
Stern _____

WHAT I LIKE IS—4

The soft white fur of a purple mitten,
The purr of a furry, purry kitten.

The gurgle of water in the sink,
The thirsty feeling when I drink.

The whir of wings, a circus clown,
A fancy shirt to wear in town.

Turtles, squirrels, and singing birds,
And verses with some clever words.

Duplicate the poem for each child. Read it with the class in unison, then ask, "Which words have the 'rrr' sound and the *e-r, i-r,* or *u-r* spelling? Underline the words. Which words rhyme? What sound does *word* have? It has an odd spelling."

THE SOUND OF *ear*—4

Duplicate these words for study and use in sentences.

ear	fear	earphone
shear	appear	hear
year	beard	gear
dear	disappear	near
clear	smear	rear
spear		

tear (also pronounced *tare*)

Eer SOUNDS LIKE *ear*—4 (ADVANCED)

cheer	pioneer	reindeer	cheerful	volunteer
engineer	deer	queer	sheer	steer

The pupils look up the words in their dictionaries, divide them into syllables, pronounce them, and use them in sentences.

Ere SOUNDS LIKE *ear*—4 (ADVANCED)

The pupils have learned *here* as a sight word early in primary grades. We point out that other words have the *ere* word part.

Paul Revere	sincere	interfere
stratosphere	atmosphere	hemisphere

The children look up the words in their dictionaries, divide them into syllables, pronounce them, and use them in sentences.

THE SOUND OF *ar*—3, 4

Words often contain *ar* pronounced like the letter *r*. Here are some words that contain the *ar* word part and may be duplicated. The pupils pronounce the words.

far	cart	yarn
card	lard	dart
arm	park	star
art	barn	shark
yard	chart	harp
bark	jar	scar
farm	mark	spark

WORKING OUT WORDS WITH *ar*— 3, 4 (ADVANCED)

These 12 words are listed for experience with syllabication, analysis, and discussion. They may be duplicated or written on the board.

marshmallow	Arkansas
harmonica	marble
garbage	barbeque
marmalade	sardine
starling	garter snake

THE HARVEST BOX—3, 4

Duplicate this story for oral reading. Ask the pupils to circle words that contain *ar*.

Grandma Carver sent a harvest box to the Hart family. It was a large box.

Karla and Charles unpacked the box. They took out sparkling red apples. There were parsnips and carrots from the garden. There were jars of marmalade and a big sack of marshmallows.

"Marvelous!" said Karla, as she took out a box of candy bars and three tins of sardines.

Charles put the wrappings in the fireplace. They all watched the flames dart. Sparks flew up the chimney.

Then they marched upstairs and went to bed. The harvest box was a great Thanksgiving gift from Grandma Carver.

WHEN *are* SOUNDS LIKE *air*—
4 (ADVANCED)

Sometimes *are* sounds like *air* as in *pair*. Make a list of these words for the children to copy, pronounce, and use in sentences.

square	bare	scare
scarecrow	warehouse	prepare
dare	fare	care
Delaware	stare	careless

WORDS WITH *air*—3, 4

1. air   2. hair   3. fair   4. pair   5. stairs   6. chair

Ask the pupils to write the numeral of the word that answers each of these questions.

Which one do we breathe? _____
Which one is on a head? _____
Which one has four legs? _____
Which one means two? _____
Which one do I climb? _____
Which one means "good weather"? _____

HOMONYMS—3, 4

The pupils may add these to their collection of homonym rhymes.

Pear-Pair

A pear is a fruit that we all like to eat.
A pair of new shoes I wear on my feet.

Bare-Bare

I wear my new shoes so my feet won't be bare.
A bear has bare feet, but he doesn't care.

Fare-Fair

A mouse dines on fare of cupcakes and cheese.
We pay fare to travel by air.
We go to the fair and we may win first prize.
Of course, we must always play fair.

140

The rhymes can be duplicated and read aloud as a group. Ask the pupils to make a list of words that have the *air* sound, a list with the *are* sound, and one with the *ere* sound. *Note:* In words like *dictionary* and *scary* the *e* is dropped.

SCARY HALLOWEEN—3, 4

Duplicate the poem or write it on the board for reading aloud. The pupils select words with the sound of *air*, underline them, and name them. They circle words that have the sound of *ear*.

We say farewell to birds and leaves.
October days are near.
Bare branches are like skeleton hands.
It's scary! I declare!
Ghosts walk around without a sound,
And pumpkins glare and stare.
Queer shapes and witches with their brooms
Go flying through the air.
Oh, Trick or Treat is fun each year.
It's spooky! So beware!
The folks prepare a candy treat,
And give what they can spare.

WORDS WITH *or*—3, 4

Write this list of words on the board and ask the pupils to use them when answering the questions.

cork   fork   horse   storm   cord   thorn

What goes with rose? _____   What goes with clouds? _____
What goes with bottle? _____   What goes with lamp? _____
What goes with knife? _____   What goes with saddle? _____

WORDS WITH *or* TO WORK OUT—
4 (ADVANCED)

Write the words in each of these four lists on the board for pupils to decode, syllabicate, and use in sentences.

uniform	New York	popcorn	morning
orchard	forty	stormy	George
torpedo	foghorn	hornet	fortune
ornament	Florida	Oregon	porcupine

These words have *ar* with the sound of *or*.

warm	quart	swarm	wart	wharf
quarter	warn	larble	reward	warp

These words have the *or* spelling but the sound of *er*.

sailor	actor	junior	governor	mirror
doctor	mayor	author	editor	director

These words have the sound of *er*.

worthless	word	worse	world	worms	work

FIND WORDS WITH *or* AND *ar* IN A STORY—3,4

Duplicate this story for silent reading. Ask the pupils to circle words that have *or* and underline words that have *ar*. They may take turns reading the story aloud.

The Porcupine

The porcupine likes the forest. The porcupine's quills are sharper than thorns. It uses the quills to protect itself if it is cornered. The quills are 2 or 3 inches long. They can dart into an animal's mouth. This can cause the animal to starve. It cannot move its mouth to eat.

One baby porcupine is born at a time. The baby has barbed, sharp quills like its mother.

THE SCHWA

Explain: "Some words begin with an *a* that is not heard plainly. It is a muffled sound. We call it a *schwa*. It is unaccented."

THE SCHWA AT THE BEGINNING OF A WORD—3, 4

Show the children several words in their dictionaries that begin with the schwa, and write the symbol on the board.

Tell them to listen for the schwa *a* in each answer of the following rhymes. (Let them know a word may have more than one schwa.) Write on the board and pronounce all the words the children will use to complete this duplicated exercise.

142

When Halloween is near,	Can you guess
Scary things _____ . (appear)	My street _____? (address)
We smelled some smoke	The dog has a bone
When we _____ . (awoke)	For himself _____ . (alone)
The cow heard a sound,	The crickets by the lake
And she looked _____ . (around)	Keep me _____ . (awake)
The mice will play	Mike and Ike
When the cat is _____ . (away)	Look just _____ . (alike)

THE SCHWA AT THE END
OF A WORD—3, 4

Write these words on the board and ask the children to use them in sentences. Listen for the schwa *a* at the end of each one.

zebra	America	banana
soda	vanilla	camera
gorilla	puma	hyena
umbrella	tuna	Della

THE SCHWA INSIDE A WORD—3, 4

When third and fourth graders use their dictionaries, they will note that all five vowels can have a schwa pronunciation. Ask them to look up these words, copy them, and use a schwa symbol (∂) instead of the vowels *a, e, i, o,* or *u.*

necklace	April	balloon
goblin	album	children
towel	nickel	ketchup
kitten	lemon	carrot
button	lettuce	minus
pencil	octopus	garden

THE SOUND OF *aw*—3, 4

List these words on a chart or on the board. Discuss the homonyms *ball* and *bawl.* Ask children to write the word that matches each of the sentences.

straw	bawl	saw	thaw	crawl
lawn	claw	draw	yawn	fawn

It is inside a scarecrow. _____
It is the sound a cow makes. _____
It means to creep. _____
It is a grassy yard. _____
You do this with a pencil. _____
It is what you do when you are sleepy. _____
It is on a bear's foot. _____
It means to melt. _____
It cuts wood (also past tense of *see*). _____
It is a young deer. _____

Au IN WORDS—3, 4

Explain that *au* and *aw* are twins. They have the same sound. Ask the pupils to work out these words. Write them on the board or duplicate them.

1. sausage	2. August	3. laundry	4. author
5. faucet	6. haunted	7. Australia	8. astronaut
9. caught	10. autumn	11. saucer	12. automobile

Then ask children to write in the space provided the numeral of the word that stands for each of the following words.

A place to wash clothes _____   Dish _____
Part of a sink _____   Meat _____
Person who goes to the moon _____   A writer _____
What you did to a ball _____   Fall _____
It is a car. It is an _____ .   Country _____
A summer month _____   Ghostly _____

MATCHING WORDS—3, 4

Duplicate the exercise. These words have the sound of *aw* as in ball. Have the children pronounce them. They write in the spaces provided the numeral of the meaning of each word.

Malted milk _____   Walnut _____
Salt _____   Walrus _____
Halter _____   Bald _____
False _____   Waltz _____

1. for a horse	2. grows on a tree	3. not true	4. a dance
5. a drink	6. no hair	7. an animal	8. goes with pepper

W FOLLOWED BY *a*—3, 4

Duplicate the exercise. When *w* is followed by *ar*, the sound is that of *aw* as in *saw*.

1. warm   2. wart   3. warship   4. warble
5. warrior   6. warn   7. wardrobe

Ask the children to write the numeral of the meaning of each word or words in the space provided.

Song of a bird _____   Fighter _____
Ship at sea _____   What traffic lights do _____
Grows on skin _____   Not cold _____
Clothing _____

All IN WORDS—3, 4

Explain that when *a* is followed by *ll*, it has the sound of *aw* as in *saw*. Write *all* on the board. Ask pupils to write these words from dictation.

fall   hall   call   tall   ball   stall   wall   all

WORD ENDINGS

WORDS THAT END WITH *y*—3, 4

Dictionaries differ on the pronunciation of final *y* at the end of a two-syllable adjective. Consult the dictionary recommended by your district. Ask individual children to write these words in sentences.

Hungry _____   Sleepy _____
Shiny _____   Funny _____
Creepy _____   Tiny _____
Juicy _____   Dusty _____
Fluffy _____   Ugly _____

Match each of the above adjectives with the appropriate noun by writing the correct numeral in each space provided.

1. pig   2. cloud   3. dot   4. peach   5. dime
6. clown   7. room   8. caterpillar   9. witch   10. baby

WORDS THAT END WITH *ly*—3, 4

Use the same procedures for these adverbs. A word should be used only once.

Loudly _____   Softly _____
Slowly _____   Brightly _____
Proudly _____   Sadly _____
Quickly _____   Tightly _____

1. The horn blew _____.
2. The ant ran _____.
3. The sun shone _____.
4. The shirt fit _____.
5. The snow fell _____.
6. The turtle crawled _____.
7. He held the flag _____.
8. The clown was sad. He cried _____.

THE *s* ENDING

If a word ends with a voiced consonant or a vowel, plural *s* has the sound of *z*. Examples: *b, d, l, m, n, r, ng, g*. The children say the rhymes with you and listen for the sound of *z*.

Swarms of bees
Are near the trees.

Alice sells
Pretty seashells.

Birds hatch from eggs.
They have weak little legs.

A bird has wings.
In spring it sings.

We can count by tens.
We can write with pens.

Do you think there are cars
On faraway stars?

Babies in cribs
Often wear bibs.

If a word ends with a voiceless consonant, plural *s* has the sound of *s*. Examples: *k, f, p, t*. The pupils say the rhymes with you and listen for the sound of *s*.

We like to take trips.
On ocean ships.

Arthur bakes
Very good cakes.

Mary Jane looks
At story books.

Usually cats
Like to hunt rats.

The reindeer's hoofs
Are on the roofs.

146

THE *es* EXTRA SYLLABLE—3, 4

If a word ends with the sound of *s, sh, ch, z,* or *x,* add *es* as an extra syllable. The pupils say the rhymes with you and hear *es,* which has the sound of *z.*

Sometimes Billy mixes
His sevens and sixes.

You must not leave wrenches
Out on park benches.

We use our noses
To smell the roses.

Rosa Lee presses
All her dresses.

Ella May races
To make all the bases.

The big fire blazes.
The baby calf grazes.

Mr. Brown wishes
To catch some big fishes.

We like to eat bunches
Of grapes for our lunches.

The little girl reaches
To get some ripe peaches.

THE FINAL *ed* ENDING—3, 4

Sometimes *ed* has the sound of *d* at the end of a word, if the word ends with a voiced consonant sound. Examples: *b, g, l, m, n, r, v, y.* Ask the children to say the rhymes with you and to supply the last word in the second line.

Flowers were smelled.
Words were _____ . (spelled)

The pet was trained.
All day it _____ . (rained)

The people dined.
Their shoes were _____ . (shined)

Boards were nailed.
Letters were _____ . (mailed)

The hole was plugged.
The pet was _____ . (hugged)

The purse was grabbed.
The robber was _____ . (nabbed)

The ladder was climbed.
The words were _____ . (rhymed)

147

A penny was saved.
A hand was _____ . (waved)

The guests all stayed,
And games they _____ .   (played)

The engine roared.
The airplane _____ .   (soared)

Ed has the sound of *t* if the root word ends with a voiceless consonant sound. Examples: *f, k, p, s.*

Two eyes blinked.
One eye _____ . (winked)

The little toad hopped,
And then it _____ . (stopped)

The pillow was fluffed.
The bag was _____ . (stuffed)

The bridge was crossed.
The yo-yo was _____ . (tossed)

The car was parked.
The poodle _____ .

WHEN *ed* IS AN EXTRA SYLLABLE—3, 4

If a root word ends with *t* or *d*, *ed* becomes an extra syllable. Ask the pupils to complete these rhymes. Duplicate them.

The bread was toasted.
The meat was _____ . (roasted)

The trombone tooted.
The barn owl _____ . (hooted)

The garden was weeded.
A hoe was _____ . (needed)

The marbles were traded.
The test was _____ . (graded)

VI

PHONICS
IN WRITING
ACTIVITIES

Writing is one of the highest functions of the human brain, for it involves many different skills, such as speech, visual recognition and recall, and language formation. Kinesthetic areas of the brain controlling motor skills, including writing, are first to develop and, therefore, are the most mature at school age. The unified process for recognizing and reproducing printed symbols is last to develop, however.

Writing, like speech and reading, eventually become automatic. Yet, in the beginning, a child writing a word must recall and recognize a wide variety of associations in the form of memory patterns and memory for sounds and configurations. Children must visualize how each of the letters *s-u-n* and the complete word appear as they write it. They use speech subvocally or even aloud as they follow the strokes of writing. The recall of motor patterns directs hand and finger movements as the letters are shaped. There is constant cooperation among the associational areas of the brain in order to produce a correctly written word.

The beginning writer may be compared to a person learning to drive a car. Initial driving efforts are a confused mixture of clutches, brakes, accelerators, and assorted knobs and levers. Arms and legs must maneuver the proper piece of equipment at the right time. Finally the driver learns to coordinate all movements into a smooth pattern of automatic response. The young writer, in first stages, has the problem of effort to make hand and fingers manipulate a pencil or crayon so that letters and words will result.

The physical energy expended in cataloging and organizing patterns and associations in the writing act will cause children to fatigue easily. Writing activities, therefore, should be limited to short periods in the early primary years.

In a rich environment, the desire to write appears long before most children have developed the maturity to master it. Usually, children who have been exposed to picture books, puzzles, crayons, chalkboards, and finger paint can write their own names upon entering school. Their senses have been activated. Their small fingers are accustomed to grasping and holding all sorts of dimensions and shapes. They are curious about the strange symbols that stand for names.

Educational experiences today present many opportunities for large- and small-muscle development, such as walking balance boards, carrying without spilling, tracing around templates, and copying forms. Thus, children today are stimulated to formal writing gradually and early as they show inclinations and abilities. Although they do not realize it, children are learning to write as they observe the teacher record the day and date of the month, the names of absent or present children, sentences other children offer, or labels for use in the classroom.

Children need many prewriting experiences to explore their newly found abilities. This means regular periods set aside for creative tactile activities. Sometimes the children should be left to their own explorations. Good motivation can cause them to accomplish a great deal of work without any supervision. But if left to their own resources, the children may reach a plateau of learning and be unable to progress farther without specific help. Instruction should be provided to build accurate perception that precludes the development of inaccuracies and poor motor habits. We may believe that, by giving a child freedom, he or she will produce something spectacular. It is more exciting, however, for children when they are motivated through stimulating ideas projected by the instructor and carefully helped along in the process. Teacher and children should discuss the strokes and their directions. Thus, visual, auditory, and verbal stimulation are all employed.

RELATING PARTS TO THE WHOLE

Calling attention to details in words so children can relate letters to the whole is an important aspect of teaching. Drawing a contour box around two words to demonstrate configuration differences enables children to visualize whole words more accurately. It would be wise to have permanent guidelines painted 4 inches apart at the bottom of the classroom chalkboard for first-grade children who write manuscript and 3-inch spacing for second- and third-grade children who are using cursive writing. Regular and consistent practice, with supervision, will be rewarded by a gradually improved product. As children write on the board, they should be encouraged to associate letter name, sound, and form. These auditory-vocal, tactile-kinesthetic-visual clues can help children remember that certain letters are tall on the guidelines: *b, d, t, l, h, k,* and *f;* some sit on the line: *a, c, e, i, o, u, m, n, r, s, w, x,* and *z;* while some letters have tails: *g, j, y, p,* and *q.*

Young children may be confused by the terms "little" and "big" letters, since some tall letters are lower-case. It is advisable to call them "capital" and "lower-case" at the onset of teaching.

WRITING ACTIVITIES AND PHONICS

This book contains an abundance of phonics activities for practicing key words, consonant sounds, consonant digraphs, and vowels; therefore, a minimum of devices and activities are included in this chapter. Emphasis, instead, is placed upon prewriting experiences, visual perception and discrimination, visualization, and recall of letter forms. It is assumed that the teacher will use these skills to develop creative writing whenever time permits and extend the many activities throughout this book to phrase, sentence, paragraph, and story composition.

READING IS REINFORCED BY WRITING

The two skills of learning to read and to write reinforce each other. Writing aids in the memory of letter forms and strengthens relationships between word parts. Writing helps children learn letters by using muscles (kinesthetic) as well as through auditory and visual avenues. The act of copying letters left to right in a word helps the children pay attention to details and to the unusual features of letters. It calls attention to reversals and other directional confusions.

Writing is an aid to teaching and learning phonics since it reinforces memory of parts or elements of words. Children tend to think of the series of sounds represented by letters they are producing. The activity of writing helps in sounding through word parts. Writing helps to fix words in children's minds. Writing accustoms children to inspect across lines, left to right, as they write, and aids their coordination of eye and hand movements.

The old saying that a child must *see* and *feel* the urge for learning a skill can be debated. As we consider the communication skills, we are aware that some children show little inclination to speak, read, or write. Those needs must be projected early. Once the stimuli have been set into motion, a need or desire that has lain dormant may suddenly blossom. Prewriting experiences can be started at kindergarten level or before. Where chalkboards are provided, children enjoy *scribbling*.

The writing activities in this chapter have been tried out with children at early primary levels. As a result, (1) the children's interest was satisfied, (2) the materials facilitated readiness to move into more formal reading and writing experiences, such as copying whole sentences, (3) the children progressed more rapidly on their own, and (4) a strong desire to read and write was cultivated.

THE TACTILE-KINESTHETIC METHOD

The following description of the tactile-kinesthetic method as a technique for implementing handwriting instruction is included here because it points up the relationship of phonics to handwriting.

Children learn to read with the eye and ear and also through their muscles. Writing or tracing letters and words enables them to bridge the gap between the visual and auditory aspects of the words and to record in their minds the patterns of the words themselves. The stimulus of movement enables them to "feel" the word progress from left to right, which is the natural way of perception.

It is surprising how many children fail to attack a word from its beginning. In the kinesthetic method, children learn a word by watching the teacher pronounce it and write it on the board. The children then look at the word, pronounce it, and trace a copy the teacher has given them. They may use one or more fingers in tracing. Having written the letter or word, the children retrace it with a pencil, repeating each letter of the word and finally the whole word. Thus, writing, spelling, and reading are all taught simultaneously. Kinesthetic practice will reduce confusion between letters having similar characteristics.

CHALKBOARD WRITING

It is suggested that children be given many opportunities to practice on a chalkboard. A number of children can do this at the same time, while the rest of the class observes or participates at the desk or table. This type of writing will develop better muscular coordination, since children will be able to use full free-arm movements. It also helps in developing left-to-right progression, because the entire body, as well as the eyes and writing arm, must move as writing proceeds across the board. Ask a custodian to saw discarded chalkboards into squares for individual use.

CHILDREN WITH LEFT-TO-RIGHT-PROGRESSION PROBLEMS

Those who study the subject of language disorders are familiar with the term "twisted symbols" (*straphosymbolia*) and a rare condition called *dyslexia* which shows itself in certain symptoms connected with reading, writing, spelling, and speech. Catherine Dreby tells us, "There are common misconceptions surrounding the subject of vision problems and reading disabilities. One is that letter and whole word reversals are symptomatic of a visual perception problem. Although this may sometimes be true, reversals may have a basis in other causes, such as stress, immaturity, and fatigue."[1]

Vision pertains to the ability of the eyes to see clearly, singly and together. An ophthalmologist can improve vision so learning can occur. *Visual perception* means a child can recognize and give meaning to visual stimuli and is able to associate visual images with sounds that go with them. Vision cannot be ignored. Although only a small percentage of children have visual problems as a cause for reading failure, physical disability cannot be ignored. The fact that clinical "dyslexia" occurs in such a few cases should not prevent efforts to understand it. Visual perception problems are often accompanied by poor eye-hand coordination. There may be an inability to see letter shapes and combinations and hear sounds, even though the child is trying hard to do so. There may be confusion in differentiating letter configurations, such as *m*, *n*, and *u* or *p*, *b*, and *d*. The child may reverse *on* and *no*, and *of* and *for*, because the design of these spellings cannot be differentiated easily. Sometimes words are substituted. The child reads a word, but a few seconds later

---

[1]Catherine Dreby, "Vision Problems and Reading Disability: A Dilemma to the Reading Specialist," *The Reading Teacher*, April 1970, pp. 788–93.

cannot visualize it in order to spell it. Numbers may be reversed, as *21* for *12*. Occasionally, the child cannot organize thoughts, follow directions, or form generalizations. If the condition is neurologically based, then the child belongs in the hands of a specialist trained in working with such disabilities.

Teachers and reading specialists will have a large number of disabled pupils who have poor visual perception. This does not necessarily mean that there is impairment in the visual associative areas of the brain. Some poor visualization can be attributable to *poor learning* or a great variety of other causes. Stanley Kreppner suggests that "visual perception can be learned."[2]

Seeing and naming letters and words does not, however, necessarily *guarantee* that a child can discriminate one letter or word from another. It is not a matter of vision, but one of *visualization*. Children must move through a period of visual adjustment before they can learn to discriminate letter forms and copy and write them. Since most of the visual problems involve consonants, consonants are taught first, then vowels. Assuming that a teacher, parent, or aide can do much to help the child who displays symptoms of poor visualization, techniques and devices are suggested in this chapter. When physical causes have been eliminated in cases of suspected reversal problems, the teacher and parent can discuss methods of helping a child to see words with accuracy.

Prewriting therapy is advised at kindergarten level so the eyes can become accustomed to moving left to right, and the process of writing and reading will become habitual. This chapter contains rhymes and other techniques dealing with directions. A kindergarten teacher can help establish left-to-right progression and prepare children for formal writing before they reach first grade or at least second grade.

○ Place pictures along the chalk rail or on the flannel board in left-to-right sequence.
○ Play "Looby-Loo" or other singing games in which the child uses left and right parts of the body.
○ Trace around templates or other figures.
○ Follow a line of print on a chart with a pointer left-to-right.
○ When a child is scribbling, direct the hand movements left-to-right.
○ Know a story so well that you can turn the book toward the class and let your finger move across the lines of print.
○ Display trade books about shapes for browsing.
○ Allow fingers to move left-to-right under a word written on the board, rather than frame the word with two hands.

---

[2]Stanley Kreppner, "On Research in Visual Training and Reading Disability," *Journal of Learning Disabilities*, vol. 4 (February 1971), pp. 66–76. *Journal of Learning Disabilities*, 101 E. Ontario St., Chicago, Ill., 60611.

○ Do not attempt to change the dominant hand.

○ Draw contour boxes around words to show contrast in shape.

○ Allow ample time for children to write a word. The letters must be written left-to-right for children to gain a full impression.

○ Teach letters that have similar parts in *pairs*, for example, *t* and *f*, *b* and *d*, with a mnemonic device so children can erase confusion.

Possible Reasons for Word Confusions

Difficulties in word perception may be the basic reason for a number of reading difficulties. Writing involves many different skills, such as listening discriminately, speaking, recognizing and recalling visual symbols, and understanding the arrangement of words in sentences. Eventually children must visualize words as wholes. To do this requires precise cooperation between associative areas of the brain and the eyes. A wide variety of systems of recall and memory patterns must operate before children can even write the strokes that make up words and before they can derive meaning from and bring meaning to an activity. There are many reasons for word confusions, among them the following.

○ *Too much emphasis upon the whole word.* If children are forced to see a whole word, they may react to a *blob*. Words that are mere configurations may mean nothing at all. Many words—adverbs, verbs, and adjectives—cannot be pictured because they are abstract.

○ *Too much emphasis upon word segments or families,* such as *ing* or *ite.*

○ *Holding the hand directly underneath a word.* Children may look at the fingertips or elsewhere for clues instead of directing the eye first to the left part of the word.

○ *Attempting to write the whole word without thinking of its parts.* Though children may "think" of a whole word, they do not write words as wholes. They write letters left to right. They must think of how letters appear and sound. Writing helps children retain an image of whole words.

○ *Lack of kinesthetic experience at kindergarten and first-grade levels.*

○ *Not clarifying letter and word problems when noted.*

Techniques to Help in Left-to-Right Orientation

LEFT AND RIGHT PARTS—K, 1

Ask children to look for objects that have left and right parts.

1. Doorknobs on a door often are on the right side. Ask, "Is our doorknob at the right?"
2. Eyeglasses have left and right parts.
3. Coats have left and right sleeves. Socks, mittens, shoes, and boots have left and right parts.

Some things are usually placed in a left or right position: knife and fork, napkin at left side of plate, return address and stamp on letter, and numerals left to right on a ruler. In the United States the steering wheel is on the left side of a bus or car.

LEFT-AND-RIGHT DEVICE—K, 1

Lay a strip of cloth along a table. Draw a partition with a felt-tip pen so there will be two equal sides. Ask children to place objects at the left or right of the division line to see if they can follow directions.

DIRECTIONS—1, 2, 3

Read two lines and ask the children to repeat them after you. As they become acquainted with the rhymes, they may say them in unison. For children who can read, duplicate the rhymes.

I move my eyes from left to right,
When I read words in a book.
I cross the street, and left to right
I always stop to look.
And when I get into the bus,
The door is at the right.
A clock's hands move around, around,
Each hour day and night.
I use both hands to type a note;
I use both left and right.
Legs in my jeans are left and right;
Sometimes they are quite tight.
I set the table for my Mom
With dishes clean and bright.
The fork is at the left, but spoon
And knife are at the right.

MY SHOE AND FOOT—K, 1

Read this poem as the children pantomime the action.

Here is my foot and here is my shoe.
Let's see if both agree.

If both shoes were left and both shoes were right,
What a problem there would be!
Show us your left shoe; show us your right;
Show us both of your shoes.
Hold out your left foot; hold out your right.
Which shoe now will you choose?

TRACING HANDS—K, 1, 2

Children ask friends to help them trace around both hands. Post the hand shapes. The next day, ask the children if they can identify their own hand shapes and write their names on them.

Read *Good Day! Which Way?*[3] to the class.

SCRIBBLING AS A PRELIMINARY STEP TOWARD WRITING

It is natural for children to express themselves with paints, crayons, and pencils, just as they have found satisfaction in braiding, working with clay, stringing beads, packing a suitcase, putting puzzles together, or any other finger, hand, small-muscle experience. Scribbling is a random experimental activity in which children learn to control their movements and even create a sense of order in what they do. The repetition is not unlike the babblings of an infant who utters the same sounds repeatedly. Handwriting is a skill that has to be learned, but it is, in fact, an extension of graphic representation—a natural ability. Very young children need little encouragement to start scribbling. If we watch a child's scribbles develop, we notice a steady progression from the stage where the pencil or crayon is first controlled to skim over a surface through a sequence of horizontal and vertical lines and clockwise and counterclockwise swirls, to the stage where a child begins to make closed shapes. Eventually, the child can lift the pencil to make lines, dots, and so on and move smoothly across a surface.

SCRIBBLE CORNER—K

Have a scribble corner where children can experiment with a wide variety of surfaces and implements: chalkboards, felt-tip pens, paints, newsprint, chalk, charcoal, and crayons. When the conventional letter shapes begin to appear among the scribbles, the child is then ready for help in producing them. Fine-muscle control is needed for beginning writing; although

---

[3]Charlotte Steiner, *Good Day! Which Way?* (New York: Knopf, 1960).

some children have this ability by the age of four, others may not until five or six.

Scribbles can be directed into more meaningful activities as children sing an adapted version of "Row, Row, Row Your Boat" and make connected rows of cursive *e*'s.

Roll, roll, roll the ball;
Roll it on the ground.
Roll, roll, roll the ball;
Round and round and round.

Children make a series of cursive *e*'s as they recite this poem.

Peel an apple very thin.
Here's the way we will begin:
Make some apple peelings now.
Here's the way. I'll show you how.

Children make small random scribbles with this rhyme.

Watch the furry little kitten
Pull the yarn from Susie's mitten.

Use the same technique:

My bicycle rolls along on its wheels.
The faster it goes, the nicer it feels!

Use the same technique, having the children make continuous up-and-down strokes in a zigzag fashion. (This is practice for slant and stick letters; note, too, that these circular movements are contained in many manuscript letters.)

Up and down, up and down,
Up and down the hill.
Up and down, up and down,
Just like Jack and Jill.

A more precise type of scribbling takes place when children have better control over movements and can even count the repetitions. Have them make continuous wavy lines with this rhyme.

Little worm makes five big humps.
She wiggles over rocky bumps.

MORE SCRIBBLES—K

Give each child a large piece of paper on which several horizontal lines have been drawn. Do not insist that the children write on the lines, although many will try to do so. They may use felt-nib markers or black crayons.

1. A truck going up and down hill. (Children draw up-and-down, connected lines as for *M*.) Preliminary practice for *A*, *K*, *k*, *N*, *V*, *v*, *M*, *W*, *X*, and *x*.
2. Railroad tracks. (Draw three or four horizontal lines under one another.) Preliminary practice for *E*, *F*, *H*, *L*, and *T*.
3. A ball rolling. (Make clockwise loops.) Preliminary practice for *D*, *B*, *b*, *h*, *m*, *n*, and *r*.
4. A plane looping the loop. (Make a series of connected cursive *e*s.) Preliminary practice for *a*, *c*, *e*, *G*, *g*, *O*, *o*, *Q*, *q*, *U*, and *u*.
5. See the lightning in the sky.
   Soon the clouds will start to cry.
   [Make zigzag lines.]
6. A laugh turns up,
   A frown turns down.
   These are two mouths
   For a clown.
   [Draw a happy and a sad mouth.]

MAKING SHAPES—K, 1

Make a triangle, one, two three:
And here's a pointed hat, you see,
A hat for an elf that I made myself.

SCRIBBLING TO MOTHER GOOSE
RHYMES—K, 1

Mother Goose rhymes recited slowly by the teacher will provide splendid rhythmic background to help children develop freedom of arm and hand movements.

FENCE POST PRACTICE
FOR STICK LETTERS—K, 1

Draw four vertical lines, leave a space, and draw four more vertical lines.

This line stands straight as straight can be.
So now we have a capital *T*. [Write *T*.]

159

IDENTIFYING LETTER STROKES
IN NAMES—K, 1, 2

Ask a child to write his or her name on the board. Then say: "Show me the curved letters in your name, the letters that have circle parts, the half circle parts, the letters with slant lines and tails."

LITTLE MOUSE—K, 1

As the teacher reads the story aloud, the aide follows the suggested movements on the chalkboard. The children listen and observe.

Once, Little Mouse wanted some cheese. She very slowly moved toward the kitchen. [Draw a long straight line horizontally.]

Just as she reached the kitchen, she heard a scratching sound. [Draw up-and-down movements.] She was frightened. Then she heard a rumbling sound. [Make a series of cursive *e*'s.] Little Mouse crept through a hole into the kitchen. She jumped and jumped to get up to the shelf. [Make upward straight lines.] She saw nothing to eat, so she jumped down. [Make vertical line.]

She heard a noise. [Make a row of humps like *m*s.] She heard a BIG noise. [Make a row of large *m* shapes.]

Little Mouse was VERY MUCH frightened. But now she knew the noises she heard were only a tree-branch scraping the window. Then she heard rain falling. [Make slanted strokes.]

Little Mouse looked out the window and saw the rain splash in puddles. [Make lower-case *j* without dot.] Little Mouse was frightened no longer. She found a piece of cheese, ate it, and fell fast asleep.

CREATIVE ACTIVITIES—K, 1

The teacher follows the instructions in these rhymes on the board, and the children copy them at their seats.

Draw some fence posts.
Make them straight.
And in between, make a gate!
[Draw an X between the posts.]

Draw a bee flying to the hive in a straight line.
Draw a grasshopper jumping.
Draw a caterpillar crawling.
Draw a bluebird flying.

Elicit children's ideas for other scribbles with meaning.

FUN WITH LETTER STROKES—K, 1

The teacher draws the lines on the board as the children draw them at their seats.

Here is a person straight and tall. [Draw vertical line.]
Here is a little one, very small. [Draw shorter line, which should be
    ignored.]
The tall one wears a long, long shoe. [Write capital *L*.]
And makes a capital *L* for you.
This is the *F* in flag, you see. [Write capital *F*.]
We add a line for capital *E*. [Write *E*.]
Two lines in *H* stand tall and straight,
A line between them makes a gate. [Write *H*.]

Ask pupils to retell the story and make the strokes as they do so.

THE LITTLE ADMIRAL—K, 1

This stroke exercise includes capital *T* and *F*; lower-case *l*, *t*, and *f*; circles; triangles; slant lines; and curves. Demonstrate each of the symbols and strokes on the chalkboard as you read the story. Read it a second time and ask the pupils to make the strokes on paper at their seats.

Once there was a little admiral. He commanded a big ship and he wore a cap. [Write capital *T*.]

One day, the little admiral took a walk. [Draw horizontal line.] He met five sailors. [Draw five vertical lines.]

The little admiral said, "Please put on your hats." And they did. [Write five lower-case *t*'s.] They all marched along together and met five ladies. Each lady wore one feather in her hat. [Write five lower-case *f*'s.] They bowed to the ladies and marched to some tents. The admiral had a tent. The five sailors each had a tent. [Draw six triangles.] They went into the tents because rain was falling. [Draw several slant lines.] It didn't stop raining, so they slept in the tents all night.

In the morning, they woke up and heard, "Mew, mew, mew." They opened the tents and saw five hungry kittens with five curled tails. [Write five lower-case *c*'s.] One sailor went out to get some milk. He fed the milk to the hungry kittens from five round dishes. [Draw five circles.]

Then the five sailors [write five lower-case *t*'s] and the admiral [write capital *T*] marched back to their ship. They each carried a flag of the United States of America. [Write five capital *F*'s.]

MANUSCRIPT WRITING

Manuscript writing was introduced in the United States in 1921. At the present time it is almost universally accepted. It is simple to teach. It requires minimal instruction since it is built upon sticks, half circles, and circles. The sticks may be slanted or slightly curved. The circles may be whole or broken, but the foundation is the same. The forms are similar to those of most typewriters, except for *g* and *a*.

Manuscript writing is legible and neat-looking because of its uniformity, and it has a lack of ostentation that gives a concise and well-arranged appearance to a whole word. These characteristics permit writing to be done with increased speed. Manuscript writing gives a child rapid feelings of success and prompts a desire to write. It also helps the child who has poor muscular coordination and the retarded reader. Manuscript writing, then, can help children to begin creative writing as soon as they have some understanding of letters and words.

THINGS TO DO—K, 1, 2

Cut capital and lower-case letters from sandpaper, flocked material, or felt, and mount them on squares of tagboard. Several publishing companies advertise letter shapes of plastic and other material.

Children close their eyes and trace a raised letter with their fingers to guess its name. Then place a plastic letter inside a sock. Children feel through the sock and try to identify the letter.

RHYMES FOR REMEMBERING
CONFIGURATIONS—K, 1, 2

Write each letter on the board as the rhymes are said. Encourage the children to learn them.

l is a stick,
t has a hat.
f has a curl
Around like that!

p has a stick and a circle,
g has a circle and tail.
[Write each of the above manuscript letters on the board as you say
    it.]

p-i-g spells a key word *pig*
And *p-a-i-l* spells *pail*.
[Write these letters.]

162

How do I remember a letter like this?
It has four slants. I cannot miss.
It is a *w* for a *wig*. [Say letter name]
Wig rhymes with *pig* and *dig* and *jig*.

h has a stick,
And a curve for you.
r's stick is small
And its curve is, too.

How do I remember *n?*
It is first in *nut*,
And last in *ten*.
[Write both words on the board and underline the letters.]

y has a tail
That is straight, you see.
Without that tail,
It would be a *v*.

TRACING LETTER FORMS

Years ago, in the rural school, teachers would write a letter or word across a carved and worn desk in chalk. The children would trace the configuration with the fingertips. Today, children have workbooks that provide a record of their achievement. Before using the workbook page, children practice writing the letter on paper, usually tracing a large letter form that the teacher has written. Sometimes the sample letters are dotted or have broken lines. The teacher provides lined paper for final practice until the children feel confident to write on the page. Although there is nothing wrong with using the word *trace*, the term *write* sometimes gives children a feeling that they are actually writing.

TRACING IN THE AIR—K, 1

Stand with your back to the class and slowly trace a letter form in the air, stopping briefly after each stroke. Children name the letter. At the beginning, list five or six lower-case forms on the board for reference. Gradually add other letter forms. Children may take turns writing letters in the air.

TEACHING LETTER FORMS

The children's attention should be drawn to the way in which the pencil moves over the paper, beginning at a certain point and following in a certain direction. This idea can create difficulty if a child has not mastered clockwise and counterclockwise movements or has not established the control necessary to lift the pencil and redirect its movements. Preciseness is unimportant. One aim at the early primary level is to teach handwriting so letter forms can be associated with name and sound.

DISCUSSION OF LETTER SHAPES—K, 1, 2

If the letter is *b*, call it by its letter name and say the word *bed* or any simple short-vowel word beginning with *b*. Second, write the letter on the board slowly so the class can observe the two different strokes. Say: "This letter is *b* ('bee'). We begin with a stick or straight line. Then we attach a circle (or half circle, depending upon the method used)." Always write the letter on the board and discuss its strokes or parts before the children attempt to trace or write it.

LETTERS THAT HAVE SIMILAR SHAPES—K, 1, 2

There is an advantage in teaching two similarly shaped letters—*m-n*, *v-w*, and *b-d*—together, for children appear to note differences more easily than similarities.

PANTOMIME *b, d,* AND *p*

With the left pointer finger and thumb, make a circle. Hold up the middle finger for a stick and you have a *b*. With the right hand, do the same for *d*. With the left hand, make a circle with the pointer finger and thumb. Add a stick with the opposite pointed finger for *p*. Suggest that the pupils try to pantomime other letter shapes with hands or body.

LETTERS WITH GUIDELINES

Draw guidelines on a chart or on the board and write the "stick" letters *l*, *t*, and *f*. Say: "Let's talk about these three letters. This one is *l* ('el'). This letter is *t* ('tee'). How is it different from *l*? How is *f* ('eff') different from *l*? Tall letters sit on the line and have no tails or curved parts." Continue the discussion with other look-alikes, such as *b*, *d*, *p*, *g*, and *q*.

SKYWRITING—1, 2

Turn your back and write an alphabet letter in the air as you say this rhyme:

See my plane fly up high
Writing letters in the sky.

The child who guesses the letter may have a turn. Use manuscript writing only. Capitals may be more easily recognized. Encourage pupils to make up their own rhymes, for example:

A, A, fly for me today.
B, B, fly high for me.

Recalling Letter Forms

Many children who confuse letter forms may be labeled as having perceptual problems because they reverse letters. While brain involvement may be a possibility, reversals are more likely due to poor writing formation. Somehow, these children never learned the exact sequence for constructing *m* and *n* or *b* and *p*. In fact, they may start both *b* and *d* with vertical lines and then make a decision to go either to the right or left to complete the letter. This decision making may cause some children to have reversal problems. Rhymes accompanying the strokes often help children recall the letter forms. The teacher can provide guidelines and directional arrows when writing these letters on the board (see "ABC Shapes," pages 169–74). Some of the key words may be different from those used in the poem on pages 108–09, yet it is well to use referral words or key words that contain short or long vowels with beginners since they are the first vowels learned. Guidelines are furnished in phonics workbooks and spellers.

BEGINNING DICTIONARY PRACTICE

WRITING NAMES—2, 3, 4

Pupils write their names in large letters horizontally, using either manuscript or cursive writing. Under each letter, they select and write words from readers beginning with the particular letter sounds that represent the consonant and vowel sounds in their name. For example, if the name happens to be *Tommy*, the child would write a list of words beginning with each letter, as: *top, to, ten; on, of, off; me, my, mother; man, mine, must;* and *you, yes, your.*

USING NAMES—3, 4 (ADVANCED)

Draw on the board a large outline of a map of the United States. Ask the children to write names of places they have visited and then to alphabetize the names.

FRAMING NAMES—K, 1, 2, 3

Write several children's names on the board and draw contour boxes around them. At the end of the day, erase the names inside the boxes. The following day, the children will find their own spaces and write their names inside.

CONSONANT ENDINGS

COMPLETE THE WORDS—2, 3

Suggest that the children refer to alphabet letters when completing these words.

be__   ca__   fa__   gu__   ha__
ja__   mo__   nu__   pi__   ra__

As an added activity, ask the children to write as many words as possible using different endings.

CONSONANT DIGRAPHS

WRITING DIGRAPHS—3, 4

Give each child a list of consonant digraphs written horizontally: *sh, ch, th, wh.* Omit *ng* and voiced *th.* As you say a word beginning with *sh* as in *shell,* the children write *sh.* Pronounce three or four words of each: *chicken, cheese, chin; show, shoe, shake; think, thumb, three; wheel, why, where.* The words may be written on the board afterward.

COMPLETING WORDS—3, 4

Duplicate incomplete words beginning or ending with one of the consonant digraphs listed above. The *ng* ending may now be included. Several

166

different words can be written for some of the incomplete words. Refer to other sections of this book where digraphs are more thoroughly detailed.

si__	__ ick	__ ell	__ umb	mat__
__ eel	__ ip	__ eese	ri__	mu__
wi__	wit__	me__	pa__	fi__

CONSONANT BLENDS

The children should be provided with words that begin with consonant blends. Refer to previous chapters for ideas on making consonant blend charts.

RIDDLES WITH CONSONANT BLENDS—3, 4

Teacher: I am looking for something that flies and begins with *p-l*. [Say letter names.]
Child: I will write *plane*.
Teacher: I am thinking of the name of an insect that begins with *f-l*.
Child: I will write *fly*.

Invite various children to be the teacher.

COMPLETING COMPOUND WORDS WITH BLENDS—4 (ADVANCED)

Duplicate a page of compound words from which blends have been omitted. The children write the correct blends. Then ask them to use the words in sentences orally.

(sn) _____ owman	(st) _____ agecoach	(sc) hop_____ otch
(sp) _____ aceship	(sm) _____ okestack	(sl) _____ owpoke
(tr) _____ eetop	(fl) _____ agpole	(bl) _____ uebird
(cl) _____ othesline	(dr) _____ agnet	(gr) _____ andfather

VOWELS

WRITE WORDS UNDER AN UMBRELLA—2, 3, 4

Draw an open umbrella shape on the board with guidelines underneath on each side of the handle. Pupils will write words from their readers containing the short-*u* vowel sound. Examples: *up, under, us, sun, nut, bug.*

TURN ABOUT—2, 3, 4

The class will enjoy turning monosyllabic words with short vowels around to see if they make sense. Here are a few starters:

net–ten	lap–pal
sub–bus	tap–pat
nuts–stun	pan–nap
dab–bad	top–pot

CROSSWORD PUZZLES—2, 3, 4

Draw a tic-tac-toe board of nine squares. Fill in the middle square. Write *cat* and *nap* horizontally and *can* and *top* vertically. Ask the children to create their own crossword puzzles using short-vowel sounds.

VOWELS IN MY NAME—3, 4

The children write first names of friends. They cross out silent vowels and underline vowels that have sounds. Remember that children's names could contain vowels that are neither long nor short, for example, *or, ar, ir, ow, oo, ou,* or a *schwa.*

WRITING VOWELS—2, 3, 4

Duplicate a list of words with missing long and short vowels. The children will write the vowel to complete each word. Ask them to cross out silent vowels. Some blanks can contain more than one vowel, so encourage the class to write as many words as possible.

c__ ke	f__ n
c__ be	p__ g
k__ te	b__ d
s__ il	b__ at
n__ t	j__ ep

ABC SHAPES

Write each letter form on the board as you say the rhyme. Then ask the children to write the letter at their seats as they recite its name.

Snipple, snapple.
An *a* for *apple*. [Draw circle.]
Pick, tick,
Make a stick. [Add stick.]

Down you go into your bed. [Stick.]
Here is a pillow for your head. [Circle.]

The children may draw a horizontal line extending from *b*. A vertical line is drawn at the end to simulate a bed. Write the word *bed* on the board and draw a contour box around it.

Here is a curve.
C is for *cat*.
See her tail
Curled around like that. [Curve.]

The children may draw a cat's face at the point where the *c* begins. Write the word *cat* on the board and draw a contour box around it.

Little raindrop
Falls to the ground. [Circle.]
The yellow *duck* likes
Its splashing sound. [Stick.]

The children may draw a duck's head and bill at the top of the vertical line. Write the word *duck* on the board and draw a contour box around it.

169

The little *elf* [Curve.]
Made a cap by himself.
[Horizontal line to form *e*.]

The children may draw an elf's ear shapes on each side to form *e*, a pointed cap on top of the letter, a face inside the lower part. Write the word *elf* on the board and draw a contour box around it.

Did you ever see
A *fish* take a stroll? [Curve and stick.]
Mine did. Then jumped
Back into its bowl. [Horizontal line.]

The children may draw a fish shape around *f*. Write the word *fish* on the board and draw a contour box around it.

Around the pen went
The billy *goat*. [Circle.]
With whiskers [Straight line and curve.]
And a shaggy coat.

The children may make two horns, an eye, and whiskers on the curved part of the letter. Write the word *goat* on the board and draw a contour box around it.

A tall feather on my *hat*; [Straight line.]
Now, down and over just like that. [Curve.]

The children draw a brim around the base of the *h*. Write the word *hat* on the board and draw a contour box around it.

I spilled the *ink*. [Straight line.]
It left a spot. [Dot.]

Write *ink* on the board and underline *i*. Draw a contour box around the word.

Down the stairs see me run [Curve.]
To get some *jam*. Yum, yum, yum!
Please do not
Forget to dot. [Dot.]

The children may pretend that *j* is a jam spoon and draw a jar shape around it. Write the word *jam* on the board and draw a contour box around it.

I want to fly
My *kite* today;
So I'll make three lines [Write *k*.]
And sail it away.

The children may draw a kite shape around the *k* and add a string. Write the word *kite* on the board and draw a contour box around it.

A little red *leaf*
Comes tumbling down; [Stick.]
It flies and whirls
All through the town.

The children may draw a leaf shape around *l* and call *l* the midrib of the leaf. Write the word *leaf* on the board and draw a contour box around the word.

Draw a stick, [Stick.]
And curves, one and two. [Two curves.]
I made a Halloween
Mask for you.

The children draw eyes inside the curves and add two strings for tying. Write the word *mask* on the board and draw a contour box around it.

Down falls a *nut*
From the walnut tree. [Straight line.]
It makes one bounce
As you can see. [Curve.]

The children may draw a nut shape around the *n*. Write the word *nut* on the board and draw a contour box around it.

Make a round *o*
Now for us. [Write *o*.]
And eight arms for
An *octopus*.

The children may add eight arms to the letter *o*. *Octopus* has three syllables, so writing the word may be deferred.

I made a stick,
Not very big, [Stick.]
And a big circle
For the face of a *pig*. [Circle.]

The children draw eyes and snout inside the curve and add two ears. Write the word *pig* on the board and draw a contour box around it.

First a big circle. [Circle.]
Then a curve comes down. [Tail.]
The *queen* wears a crown
And a trailing gown.

The children may say the last two lines as they write lower-case *q*. They may draw a crown on top of the *q* and a face inside the curve. Write the word *queen* on the board and draw a contour box around it.

The little *rat* hides
Behind the wall, [Stick.]
Shows part of its tail,
And that is all. [Curve.]

The children say the verses as they write *r*. Write the word *rat* on the board and draw a contour box around it.

Two neat curves we'll have to make, [Write *s.*]
And here's a little curled-up snake.

The children may want to draw heads on their "snakes" and write a row of *s*'s coming from the mouth.

My *top* spins around [Stick.]
With a spinning sound. [Cross *t.*]

The children may draw a top shape from the horizontal line to a point. Write the word *top* on the board and draw a contour box around it.

U for *umbrella* [Curve.]
Makes a cup [Stick.]
If you forget
To put it up!

The children may draw a handle at the top of *u* and a point beneath to simulate closed umbrella. Write *umbrella* on the board and draw a contour box around it.

Valentine hearts
Have a point, you see,
Just like the one
On the letter *v.* [Two slant lines.]

The children may make the *v* into a *valentine.* Write the word on the board and draw a contour box around it.

Ocean *waves* [Slant line.]
Move like this, [Slant line.]
A sight you do not [Slant line.]
Want to miss. [Slant line.]

The children make a row of *w*s. Write the word *waves* on the board and draw a contour box around it.

To end the word *box*
Here's what to do:
Cross some sticks,
One and two. [Write X.]

Write *box* on the board and underline *x*. Draw a contour box around the word.

A slant line first, [Slant line.]
And then a tail. [Tail.]
Here is a *yo-yo*.
Make it sail!

The children may draw a yo-yo shape at the top of the *y*. Write the word *yo-yo* on the board and draw a contour box around it.

Zebra, zebra has many
Stripes of black,
Zig, zag, zig [Write *z*.]
Along its back.

Write the word *zebra* on the board and draw a contour box around it.

LEARNING AND IMPROVING THE SOUNDS OF ENGLISH

Today our schoolchildren come from a big variety of ethnic groups. In one California county, over 80 different languages are spoken, among them Japanese, Korean, several Chinese dialects, Filipino (Tagalog), Spanish, Arabic, Lithuanian, Cambodian, Albanian, Norwegian, and Vietnamese. The numbers of these children have increased year by year. Many of these children arrive at the education center with little or no knowledge of the English language and have had few experiences to relate to what is said. Many come from rural villages where they received little or no previous schooling. New arrivals may present unusual language problems: Their native language does not contain many of the English sounds. Teachers of non-English-speaking

175

children express concern about how to help their charges become English speakers, readers, and writers.

Teachers should not be dismayed when the newcomers' beliefs and values run contrary to their own. Nor can teachers possibly have a knowledge of the religious customs, dietary differences, and family life of each individual child. Education of bilingual children does not mean separateness: rather, it relates individuals to others. These children *want* to become successful members of a new society; therefore, teachers will do their utmost to help in the adaptation process.

Some programs advise that children speak and read in their native language first. Other programs recommend a language-experience approach. Most teachers find they must offer a wide variety of learning skills. Each approach tries to help overcome, in some way, the problems presented by language differences.

Often, it is difficult to secure teachers who are competent in two to say nothing of several languages. Parents' help is needed more and more. Parents sometimes serve as uncredentialed aides and interpreters. Many of them are themselves desirous of learning to speak fluent English.

Children who have difficulty in understanding English are at a disadvantage and suffer multiple hindrances and embarrassments when they cannot deal with incoming verbal clues. They must cope not only with one language learned at home, but often with an argot or substandard one in the community, as well as a standard and more socially acceptable one at school.

A great culture shock occurs when a little child suddenly is plunged into a new way of speaking. One-word expressions, gestures, and jargon understood by peers are no longer acceptable. One way of helping non-English-speaking children to express feelings through language is to encourage forms of play that will promote egocentric speech, and let the children use their native language to explain what is being done. If these children are completely withdrawn, it is necessary for a sensitive bilingual person to talk with them. The child who has little or no ability to speak English usually is helped in special classes. It is important, however, for the teacher to understand which sounds the child has difficulty in producing and to concentrate upon those particular sounds in teaching phonics. Time should be arranged so that all these children are brought together and correct patterns are taught to the group as a whole through the poems, exercises, and stories in this book.

It is impossible, in a phonics book of this size, to include exercises that will be a source of transition material for all languages. Spanish has therefore been selected as the language on which to base practice materials. The exercises in this book, however, lend themselves to adaptation and should help any child with a need to learn a second language.

HELPING SPANISH-SPEAKING CHILDREN

Spanish-speaking children, in addition to confusing tenses and making other grammatical errors, have difficulty with sounds, some of which do not occur in their own native language. Speaking may be no fun for them, for often they cannot manage either Spanish or English very well.

Some reasons for their difficulty include the following:

○ There is no *z* in a final position in Spanish. The speaker may substitute *s* for *z*. See chapter V for help in this instance.
○ There is no schwa in Spanish.
○ Spanish does not ordinarily permit a cluster of consonants plus *s* in the same syllable, and a child may substitute *es* for *s*, as in *topes*.
○ The possessive suffix is absent. Ask the children to say, "The pen of Jack" and then "Jack's pen."

There is no trouble in producing:

○ Long *e* as in feet
○ Short *e* as in *pet*
○ *or* as in *port*
○ Short *u* as in *nut*

The special teacher who uses this book will concentrate on sounds with which the Spanish-speaking child has difficulty. The teacher will include those sounds in auditory, speech, reading, and writing practice.

Auditory Practice

VOWELS

It is important that Spanish-speaking children have vowel practice, particularly with vowels that are difficult to differentiate aurally. Ask the children to say the words after you. Mouth positions are important; for example, ask the children to smile when long *e* is said, round the lips for *oo*, and open the mouth for *ar* and short *u*. Say, "Watch my mouth when I say these words."

seat–set	cart–cut	soup–sup	lard–lord
meat–met	boot–but	heart–hut	bard–board
Pete–pet	root–rut	card–cord	mark–mutt
beat–bet	coop–cup	hard–hoard	

177

Difficult vowels include the following:

The schwa: above, around, sofa (sounds like short *u*: cup, bun)
Short *i*: it, sit, mill, fin, win
Short *a*: apple, sat, cat, map, pat
aw: caught, bought, paw, saw, jaw

See the explanation of vowels and the extensive lists of words on pages 183–93.

DIFFICULT CONSONANTS

Ask the children to watch your mouth as you say these words with difficult consonants. They say each word after you.

v: have, over, save, very, cover, glove
th (voiceless): thank, think, bath, path, thin
th (voiced): that, this, these, those, father
sh: shoe, shell, dish, wish, fishbowl
z: isn't, zoo, was, pans, zipper
m (final position): time, home, come, some
r: run, read, carrot, car, red
j: jam, jump, bridge, engine, jeep
zh: treasure, pleasure, garage
h: hat, house, his, hen, hand

THE SCHWA *a*

Start with short *u* as in *sun* and practice *run*, *fun*, *bug*, *rug*, and *umbrella*. Transfer to the unaccented schwa and clap for each syllable, as in *a-round* and *a-lone*, accenting the last syllable. Clap hard on the last syllable. Explain that the sound of *a* is made like a soft grunt ("uh"). Children who can use a dictionary should look up the words and note the symbol for the schwa.

Practice with the schwa *a* in initial position:

around: around the house	The cat runs around the house.
alone: all alone	The dog is all alone with a bone.
above: above the tree	The nest is above in the tree.
agree: agree with you	I agree with you.
away: ran away	The puppy ran away.
alive: is alive	The baby bird is alive.
asleep: fall asleep	I fall asleep at night.

alike: are alike   The two goats are alike.
across: across the room   See me walk across the room.
America: sing "America"   "Sing 'America, the Beautiful.'"

THE SCHWA IN DIFFERENT WORD POSITIONS

Practice with the schwa *a* in the final position. Clap out the syllables in each word, making a loud clap on the accented syllable.

China	panda	mama	Arizona	camera
Alaska	Anna	banana	puma	zebra
hyena	vanilla	Santa	Rosa	gorilla
hula	sofa	Papa	umbrella	soda
Alabama	Garcia	comma	Montana	tuna

OTHER VOWELS WITH THE SCHWA SOUND

Explain that a schwa can be located in any part of the word. In the following lists, all vowels are represented as schwas. The schwa is almost "swallowed" when we say *pencil.* Continue to clap out the syllables.

a: necklace, balloon, metal
e: vowel, kitten, nickel
i: goblin, pencil, April
o: button, lemon, carrot
u: lettuce, octopus, minus

Appendix I defines the schwa. Other exercises for schwa practice are on pages 142–45 and 189.

SHORT *I* AND SHORT *E* DISCRIMINATION

Spanish-speaking children may say *peen* for *pin* since short *i* is not a part of their native language. Ask each of these questions and invite individual children to tell which word is correct. Ask them to smile when they pronounce long *e.*

Do we fasten things with a *peen* or a *pin?*
Can you cover a pan with a *lid* or a *lead?*
Is an animal a *peeg* or a *pig?*

179

Is an elephant *beeg* or *big?*
Can you *leek* or *lick* an ice cream cone?
If you eat too much, do you get *seek* or get *sick?*
Do you eat a potato *cheep* or a potato *chip?*
Do you have a *heel* or a *hill* on your foot?
Can you ride on a *ship* or a *sheep?*
Which one is an animal, a *sheep* or a *ship?*

THE SOUND OF *AW*

The children pronounce these words after you:

caw	draw	bawl
crawl	stalk	yawn
jaw	straw	fall
walk	chalk	hawk
paw	lawn	wall
talk		

Then they answer these questions in complete sentences:

Can you talk? (Yes, I can talk.) Can you walk?
Do you have a jaw? Where is your jaw? Can a man saw wood?
Can a baby crawl? What else can crawl? Do you yawn?
When do you yawn? Can you draw a picture? Does a dog have paws?
Does a chicken have claws? What is a lawn? Does a lawn have grass?
Do you write with chalk? Where do you write with chalk?
When do leaves turn color? (fall, autumn)

THE LETTERS *b, d,* AND *r*

The letters *b, d,* and *r* are pronounced differently in English than in Spanish. Ask the children to use a mirror for observing and a tape for listening to their own production. Comparing their practice with a correct model is suggested.

The teacher is advised to turn to sections in this book that provide practice with these sounds.

Sh-ch

Spanish-speaking children may substitute *ch* for *sh* and the reverse, *sh* for *ch*. Since *sh* does not occur in their language, they confuse the sounds. Also, their *ch* is not as pronounced as the English *ch*.

Work with comparisons such as:

sip–ship	seep–sheep	so–show
Sue–shoe	sop–shop	sell–shell

Finally, practice lists of words beginning with *sh* and *ch*. Give auditory practice so children can hear the difference. For example:

chip–ship	chin–shin	chop–shop
choose–shoes	chill–shill	chew–shoe

SUGGESTIONS FOR SPEECH IMPROVEMENT

Here are speech-correction ideas that the specialist, teacher, or parent may use when helping a child to pronounce a speech sound correctly within context.

VOWELS

around, bun: For *a* and *u* start with the *ah* in *padre* or in the English *father* and raise the jaw for *uh*.

it, sit: For *i* start with a big smile while producing Spanish *i* as in *bigota* or long *e* in *bee*, and gradually release the smile.

sat, apple: For *a* start with the *a* as in *padre* and in the English *father* and raise the jaw slightly while you smile.

cough, saw: For *ou* and *a* start with the Spanish *o* as in *bota* and drop the jaw, but keep the lips rounded.

CONSONANTS AND CONSONANT DIGRAPHS

very, have, cover: For *v* start with *f* and add voice volume.

thank, both, toothbrush: For the voiceless *th* put out the tongue between the teeth and blow. Voice is quiet.

thin, thick, bathe, father: For the voiced *th* same as voiceless *th*, but use the voice.

hat, hen: For *h* like initial *g* in Spanish; *h* is silent in Spanish *hora*.

shoe, wishbone: For *sh* place finger beside mouth as if to say "be quiet"; say "sh" in isolation.

zoo, buzzard, fuzz, isn't, bells: For *z* and *s* start with "ssss" or a hiss and add voice.

me, time, hum: For *m* start with a sentence, "See *my* hand," and prolong the "mmmm" in *my*.

run, carrot, car: For *r* place tongue tip in back of the mouth. Curl up the tongue tip.

jam, bridge, engine: For *j* and *g* start with *ch* and gradually add voice volume.

THE EXAGGERATED "ssss" SOUND

Spanish-speaking children are likely to add short *e* to an *s*, as in *estop*. Prolong the "ssss" sound.

HUM AWHILE

Ask the children to hum at the end of each of these words:

ham	hum	him	time
Sam	crumb	dime	home
drum	rhyme	stem	lamb
climb	comb	thumb	broom
come	jam	team	room

Turn to the section in this book that emphasizes the sound of *m*.

THE APOSTROPHE

Tell the children to say these sentences after you.

The tail of the cat is long. The cat's tail is long.
The shirt of Jack is new. Jack's shirt is new.
An ape has an ugly face. An ape's face is ugly.
The handle of the mop is long. The mop's handle is long.
The wool of a sheep is thick. A sheep's wool is thick.
The bark of a dog is loud. A dog's bark is loud.
The flag has red and white stripes. The flag's stripes are red and white.
The bill of a hen is sharp. A hen's bill is sharp.
The engine of a car makes it go. A car's engine makes it go.
The girl has a pretty face. The girl's face is pretty.
The rays of the sun are warm. The sun's rays are warm.
The kite has a long string. The kite's string is long.
The tail of a pig is curly. A pig's tail is curly.
The story by Jane was excellent. Jane's story is excellent.
A tiger has black stripes. The tiger's stripes are black.

VOWELS

This section on vowels is included because many dialectal groups have difficulty with them. This book has emphasized consonants so far because they are more frequently misarticulated than vowels by English-speaking children and they represent more visual problems. Every word must have a vowel, however. It is important for the teacher and parent to understand how the vowels are produced.

A vowel is a voiced sound made by allowing the breath stream to pass unobstructed through the mouth. It is modified by the shape of the mouth and the position of the tongue. Every word contains a vowel. The extent of the mouth opening varies with the production of the vowel. The elevation of the tongue and the movement of the jaw go together.

In order to produce a vowel sound correctly, it is necessary to know (1) how the mouth is shaped, and (2) where and how much the tongue is raised or if the tongue tip rests behind the lower front teeth.

Front Vowels

These are made with intrinsically the same mouth and tongue positions. The lips are spread in a smile for all front vowels.

E-e (LONG): *e* AS IN *me* AND *see*

The children smile with the lips. The teeth are slightly apart. The sides of the tongue are raised slightly, or the tongue tip can lie flat behind the lower teeth. The children distinguish between these words:

bed–bead	did–deed	bit–beet	dip–deep
ten-teen	ken–keen	pill–peel	dill–deal

Then they can repeat these long-*e* words in the initial position:

each	eagle	easy	eat	eel
easel	Easter	equal	eaves	east

Let them use some of the words in sentences; for example:

Two plus two *equal* four.
An *eagle* is a bird.
Let's hunt *Easter* eggs.
We *eat* vegetables.
East is the opposite of west.
We have an *easel* in this room.

The children can then repeat these one-syllable words ending in *e:*

be	we	free	flea	three
knee	tree	see	he	she
me				

I-i (SHORT): *i* AS IN *ink* AND *igloo*

The children smile. The teeth and lips are a little farther apart than for *e* as in *me*. The tongue tip is behind the lower teeth. The front of the tongue is raised toward the roof of the mouth and a little farther back than for *e*. Ask the children to distinguish between these words:

beg–big	pen–pin	peg–pig	big–beg
fell–fill	pick–peck	hem–him	tell–till

Then they can repeat these words with *i* in the initial position:

if	in	ill	ink	inch	igloo	is	itch	into

Let them use some of the words in sentences; for example:

The puppy *is ill.*
I put flowers *into* the box.
A pen holds *ink.*
Flowers are *in* the box.
This *is* a box.
Something makes me *itch.*

E-e (SHORT): *e* AS IN *end* AND *every*

The children smile slightly. Teeth and lips are a little farther apart than for *i* as in *inch*. The front of the tongue is raised toward the roof of the mouth a little farther back than for *i*. Ask the children to distinguish between these words:

bag–beg	shall–shell	tan–ten	lag–leg
pan–pen	sat–set	mat–met	had–head

Then they can repeat these words with *e* in the initial position:

end	engine	elk
else	enter	egg
elephant	extra	

184

Let them use some of the words in sentences; for example:

An *elephant* is a large animal.
An *engine* pulls a train.
An *elk* has big horns.
The hen lays an *egg*.

A-a (SHORT): *a* AS IN *ant* AND *apple*

The children smile. Teeth and lips are much farther apart than for *e* as in *end*. The front of the tongue is raised toward the roof of the mouth farther back and lower than for *e*. The mouth is open more widely than for *e*. Ask the children to distinguish between these words:

bag–beg–big
pen–pan–pin
pet–pat–pit
met–mat–mitt

Then they can repeat these words with *a* in the initial position:

add	as
ax	apple
ant	animal
am	at
an	ashes

Let them use some of the words in sentences; for example:

The *ant* is an insect.
A cat is an *animal*.
An *apple* is a fruit.
We *add* two plus two.

Back Vowels

A-a ("ah"): *a* AS IN *car*

The mouth is wide open. Ask the children to place two fingers between the teeth to determine width of the mouth opening. The tongue is slightly raised. Ask the children to distinguish between these words:

cart–court	barn–born	part–port
far–for	scar–score	tar–tore

Then they can repeat these words with *a* (*ar* in the initial position):

are   arm   art   arch   army
ark   arbor   argue   Arnold   marched

Let them use some of the words in sentences; for example:

We *are* learning sounds.
I have more than one *arm*.
We have *art* and draw pictures.
An *army* of people *marched*.

O-o (SHORT): *o* AS IN box AND *stop*

The mouth is rounded and more nearly closed than for *a* as in *arm*. The mouth is pulled in at the corners. The back of the tongue is raised slightly. The children distinguish between these words:

Dan–Don   cap–cop
rat–rot   hat–hot
cat–cot   shack–shock
pat–pot   gnat–not

Then they can repeat these words with *o* in the initial position:

otter   ox
odd   octave
octopus   olive
object

Let them use some of the words in sentences; for example:

An *otter* swims in the sea.
An *octopus* has eight arms.
An *olive* is good to eat.
An *ox* pulled a covered wagon.

Note: Words containing *o* with two pronunciations or words with the *aw* sound (*hog*, *moss*) are not included.

A-a ("aw"): *a* AS IN yawn AND *awful*

The mouth is very round and more nearly closed than for *o* as in *not*. The lips protrude and are rounded slightly. The back of the tongue is raised.

The children distinguish between these words:

tot–taught	yon–yawn
sod–sawed	Don–dawn
hock–hawk	cot–caught
pod–pawed	pon–pawn

Then they can repeat these words with *a* ("aw") in the initial position:

all   auto   also   awful   off   office

They repeat these words with *a* ("aw") in the medial position:

lawn   dawn   because   walk   walrus   sauce   caught

Let them use some of the words in sentences; for example:

The *lawn* has grass.   A *walrus* lives in the sea.
Ha *caught* a fish.   Let us take a *walk*.

Oo (SHORT): DOUBLE *oo*
AS IN *wool* AND *good*

The mouth is rounded and more nearly closed than for *a* as in *yawn*. The lips protrude and are relaxed. The back of the tongue is raised high. Have the children distinguish between these words:

pull–pool	would–wooed
full–fool	should–shooed
stood–stewed	could–cooed

Then they pronounce these words and use them in sentences. Example: We cut *wood* for the fireplace.

wood	hood	cook	book	wool	brook	crooked
shook	nook	shook	took	good	foot	woodpecker

Oo (LONG): DOUBLE *oo*
AS IN *cool* AND *food*

The lips are rounded, nearly closed, and they protrude. The back of the tongue is raised high. Use the exercises on pages 130–33 in which the children distinguish between long and short *oo*.

The children say *oo* in final position:

blue	coo	moo	who	too	Sue
zoo	grew	flew	boo	two	

Then let them use the words in sentences; for example:

The ghost said, "*Boo.*"
Two is a number.
Birds *flew* away.
A color is *blue.*

Middle Vowels

R ("er"): *r* AS IN *fern*,
bird, AND *turn*

The lips are relaxed. The tip of the tongue is raised and curled back slightly. The middle of the tongue is raised. *R* is modified by vowels *e*, *i*, and *u*. This sound is pronounced differently in various regions of the United States. The children distinguish between these words:

wed–word	ben–burn
wood–word	stood–stirred
peck–perk	hood–heard
shut–shirt	

They pronounce the "er" sound in the initial position:

early	earn	earth	Earl	fern	burn

Then let them use some of the words in sentences; for example:

We live on the *earth.*
A *fern* is a plant.
His name is *Earl.*
Don't *burn* yourself.

U-u (SHORT): *u* AS IN *up* AND *uncle*

The lips are in a relaxed position. The tongue is raised slightly back of the center. The tip is against the lower front teeth. Have the children distinguish between these words:

cot–cut   not–nut   pop–pup   hot–hut   bog–bug

They pronounce the sound of *u* in the initial position:

ugly   uncle   under   until   us   up   unless   upstairs

A-a (SCHWA): THE SCHWA SOUND
IN *about* AND *around*

This is an unaccented sound. Sometimes it is called the *grunted* sound, as in "uh." The children practice these words with the schwa in the initial position:

alive	attack	awake	about
annoy	asleep	allow	amaze
along	ago	awhile	account

Then they practice these words with the schwa in the final position:

gorilla	banana	soda	vanilla	zebra
arena	camera	China	puma	tuba

They practice these words with the schwa in the medial position:

alphabet (*a*)   arithmetic (*a* and *e*)
accident (*e*)   circus (*u*)
balloon (*a*)   breakfast (*a*)

Finally, use some of the words in sentences.

Diphthongs

A diphthong is a combination of two pure vowels. It is a glide sound made with the tongue starting in the position for one vowel and moving immediately toward another vowel position.

A-a (LONG): THE *a* DIPHTHONG

The children begin with short *e* and glide toward short *i*. They distinguish between these words:

back–bake	pan–pane	rack–rake	ran–rain
pan–pain	man–mane	hat–hate	can–cane
fat–fate	mat–mate	tack–take	Jack–Jake

189

They pronounce these words beginning with the *a* diphthong:

ape   ace   age   angel   apron   ache   ate   acre

Ask children to make sentences using some of the words beginning with the *a* dipthong; for example:

My sister wears an *apron*.
An *angel* is on top of the Christmas tree.
An *ape* is in a cage at the zoo.
The bird *ate* a seed.

Next they pronounce words ending in the *a* diphthong:

may	play	gray	way
bay	obey	Jay	lay
hay	day	say	stay
they	away	pay	neigh

Finally, they make sentences using some of the words ending with the *a* dipthong. Ask: "Can you make a sentence that contains three of the words?"

I-i (LONG): THE i DIPHTHONG

The children begin with "ah" and glide toward short *i* quickly. They should not prolong the second sound as "ee." Ask them to distinguish between:

din–dine	pin–pine
hid–hide	shin–shine
fin–fine	lid–lied
lick–like	kit–kite

They pronounce words beginning with the *i* diphthong:

ice	iron	island	eye	ivy
icicle	idle	ivory	iceberg	

Then ask them to make sentences using some of the words beginning with the *i* dipthong; for example:

Ivy is a plant.   An *island* is in the sea.   *Ice* is cold.
You have more than one *eye*.
    (Discuss the spelling of this word.)

Next they pronounce words ending with the *i* diphthong:

by	lye	tie	sky	cry
spy	my	high	pie	why

Finally, they make sentences using some of the words ending with the *i* diphthong. Ask: "Can you use two of the words in one sentence?" Write the words on the board.

O (DIPHTHONG): THE *o* DIPHTHONG

The children begin with *o* and glide to short *oo*. Have them distinguish between words that have no diphthongs:

cot–coat   not–note   cod–code   got–goat   rod–road

Then they distinguish between the "aw" sound and the *o* diphthong:

bought–boat	bawl–bowl
caught–coat	paws–pose
call–coal	fawn–phone

They pronounce words beginning with the *o* diphthong:

oak	oatmeal	old	open
over	oval	ocean	own

Next they pronounce words ending with the final *o* diphthong:

go	no	grow	crow	throw
low	so	toe	know	hello

Finally, they make sentences after discussing the meanings of the words listed.

Oi-oy (DIPHTHONG):
THE *oi* (*oy*) DIPHTHONG

The children begin with the lips rounded and protruded for "aw" and glide quickly to short *i*. They differentiate between:

tall–toil	jaw–joy
lawn–loin	ball–boil
fall–foil	gnaws–noise

They pronounce words with *oy* in final position:

boy   toy   enjoy   destroy
Roy   joy   employ   annoy

Then they pronounce words with *oi* in medial position:

boil   coil   noise   voice   coin
point   soil   foil   toil

Finally, let them make sentences after discussing word meanings. Ask: "Name something you might *boil*. Would you *employ* a *boy*? Name a noisy *noise*. Name a quiet *noise*. *Point* to your *voice* box in your neck. Name an insect that might *destroy* a crop. What do you *enjoy* doing?"

Ow (*ou*) DIPHTHONG:
THE *ow* (*ou*) DIPHTHONG

The children begin with "ah" and glide quickly to short *oo* as in *wood*. They should avoid starting with short *a*. Ask them to differentiate between:

gun–gown   muss–mouse
ton–town   hull–howl
shut–shout   putt–pout

Then they distinguish between:

pot–pout   spot–spout
Dan–down   Nan–noun
got–goat   shot–shout
lad–loud   dun–down

They pronounce words beginning with the *ow* diphthong:

out   ouch   owl   our   ounce

Next they pronounce words ending with the *ow* diphthong:

cow   allow   how   now   bough
brow   plow   sow   eyebrow

Finally, let them make sentences after they have discussed the meanings of the words.

U-u (DIPHTHONG): THE u DIPHTHONG

The children begin with short *i* and end with long *oo*. Have them differentiate between:

whose–hues   coo–cue   coot–cute   mood–mewed   food–feud

They pronounce words with the *u* diphthong in the initial position:

use   unit   you   you'll   youth   union

Then they pronounce words with the *u* diphthong in the final position:

few   mew   view   cue   review

Next they differentiate between:

cut–cute   cub–cube   hug–huge

Finally, ask them to repeat these sentences:

The *cute* kitten *mewed.*
Utah is a state.
An elephant is *huge.*
The rose is *beautiful.*
A *cube* has six sides.
We have a nice *view* from the window.
We like *music.*
A *mule* is an animal.

Appendices
Index

GLOSSARY

Analytic method: Word, phrase, and sentence method of teaching reading.

Antonym: One of a pair of words of opposite meaning.

Articulation: The act of uttering speech sounds.

Articulatory defects: Substitution, omission, addition, or distortion of speech sounds.

Attention span: The time limit during which a child can pay attention.

Auditory acuity: Keenness of aural impressions caused by transmissions of impulses by the eighth cranial nerve to the brain.

Auditory discrimination: The ability to differentiate between pitches or intensities of sounds.

Auditory identification: The ability to discern sounds in various positions within words.

Basal words: Words common to a particular series of readers.

Blend: The fusion of two or more speech sounds, each of which maintains its identity.

Cognates: Sounds that are pronounced intrinsically alike by the speech organs, except that one sound is voiced and the other is voiceless, e.g., *b-p* and *t-d.*

Communication: Expression conveyed through listening, speaking, reading, and writing.

Comprehension: Understanding of concepts.

Configuration: General form of a letter or word.

Consonant: Any speech sound in which the expired breath stream is blocked, stopped momentarily, or diverted during its production; any letter sound of the alphabet, except *a, e, i, o, u,* and sometimes *y* (*my*). In *grow,* the *w* acts as a vowel but is not sounded.

Consonant blend: The fusion of two or more consonant speech sounds, each of which maintains its identity.

Consonant digraph: Two letters that produce one sound, e.g., *sh, zh.*

Continuant sound: One that can be prolonged without distortion. Examples: *s, sh, f, h, l, m, n, r, v, z.*

Decoding: Pronouncing letter sounds, words, phrases, or sentences when seen in written or printed form

Diphthong: A gliding sound produced by moving the speech organs from one vowel position to another, e.g., *ow, oy.*

Encoding: Putting letters, words, phrases, and sentences into written form.

Graphemes: Written letters representing spoken sounds.

Homograph: One of two or more words that are spelled the same but have different vowel sounds, e.g., *bow.*

Homonym: One of two or more words that have the same sound but different meanings and sometimes different spellings.

Identification: Locating a sound within a word.

Initial consonant: The beginning consonant sound in a word.

Intonation: The systematic rhythms and melodies of spoken English.

Juncture: Pause.

Key word: A word in which a certain consonant, vowel, or phonogram serves as a recall tool when a child attempts to decode a similar word.

Kinesthetic: Pertaining to or describing motor sensations.

Larynx: The voice box.

Lateral lisp: A speech defect caused by air spilling over the sides of the tongue, resulting in "slushy" pronunciation of such letter sounds as *s, z, sh, zh, ch,* and *j.*

Lip reading: A skill that enables an individual to understand what is being said by watching lip movements, expressions, and gestures. (Also known as *speech reading.*)

Listening: A process of eliciting ideas from a speaker's vocalized symbols through concentration and attention.

Macron: A line placed over a vowel to indicate the long sound, e.g., *cāke.*

Medial consonant: A consonant sound inside the word.

Monosyllabic word: A word of one syllable.

Morphemes: Special characteristics of a word: its parts, suffixes and prefixes, inflectional endings, e.g., *es,* or *ed* in *begged.*

Motor-kinesthetic (sometimes *moto-*): Pertaining to sensations in the mouth, nose, and throat as speech is produced.

Nasals: Three consonant sounds: *m, n,* and *ng.*

Objective: An end of behavior apprehended or anticipated as a perception or conceived as an idea about the child.

Participation: The degree to which a person appears to enter into and react to a situation.

Phoneme: A single sound of spoken language.

Phonetic analysis: The separation of words into those letters and combinations of letters that are associated with the sounds of speech.

Phonetics: A scientific study of speech sounds; the discrimination, identification, and production of these sounds.

Phonics: An application of phonetics (see above) to reading, writing, and spelling; use of alphabet symbols and configurations of letters and words; blending of sounds into words.

Phonogram: A phonic element that does not make a word in itself, e.g., *ight, ote.*

Phrase: A group of words that expresses a thought but lacks a predicate or perhaps a subject.

Plosive: A speech sound produced by stopping the breath stream momentarily, then releasing the breath with an explosive puff: *p, b, t, d, k, ch, j, g;* also *explosive.*

Polysyllabic word: A word consisting of many or more than three syllables.

Prefix: One or more letters or syllables added to the beginning of a word to change its meaning.

Pronunciation: The way in which words are accented and enunciated.

Reading readiness: A particular stage of maturation in which a child is able to approach the reading process and begin to acquire meaning from printed symbols (letters and words) with a minimum of frustrations and negative effects.

Root word: An original word form, to which prefixes and suffixes are added.

Schwa: An unaccented or subdued sound, as in *a*round or Chin*a.*

Semi-vowel: A speech sound, such as *l* or *r,* that has the characteristics of a consonant and a vowel. It is an arbitrary classification used by some phoneticians.

Sentence pattern: The order of words and parts of a sentence.

Sight word: A word that a child learns by sight without consideration for word elements or analysis of parts.

Speech correction: Remediation of abnormal speech that calls attention to itself and interferes with communication.

Speech defect: A disorder of speech that results from substituting, omitting, distorting, or adding sounds, due to functional or organic reasons.

Speech development: A process of speech acquisition measurable by certain norms of comparison: sounds learned, sentence length, vocabulary size, etc.

Speech improvement: The type of training given to those within a wide range of the normally adequate as well as to those in the process of speech development to ensure that speech progresses normally.

Stress: Emphasis.

Structural analysis: Visual scrutiny of the total word form to determine its structural pattern.

Substitution: Replacement of a letter or group of letters in order to make a new word, e.g., taking *c* from *cake* and substituting *t* to make *take.*

Suffix: One or more letters or syllables added to the ending of a word to change its meaning.

Syllabication: Dividing words into syllables according to a standard dictionary.

Synonyms: Words that have intrinsically the same meaning.

Syntax: The way in which words are put together to make a phrase, clause, or sentence.

Synthetic method: Combining letters, sounds, and syllables to form words. Isolation of elements in a word so the children can hear individual sounds or phonograms.

Tactile-kinesthetic: Pertaining to sensations in the fingers during the act of feeling, tracing, or writing.

Visual acuity: Gaining a series of impressions from the printed page as the eyes move across a line of print.

Visual perception: A cognitive process by which visual impressions become meaningful in the light of the individual's past experiences and present needs. This perception occurs after visual impressions have been decoded and their meanings recognized.

Voiced consonant: A consonant that requires vocal cord vibration: *d, g, j, l, m, n, r, v, w, y, z.*

Voiceless consonant: A consonant that requires no vocal cord vibration; *f, h, k, p, s, t.*

Volume: Degree of loudness.

Vowel: A voiced speech sound in which the vocal sound is modified as it passes through the throat and the head cavities. Different vowels are produced by changing the shapes of the cavities and by varying the tongue position.

Vowel digraph: The glide of one vowel to another as "aw"–short *i* (*oy*) or "ah-oo" (*ow*).

Writing, kinesthetic: See *Kinesthetic.*

APPENDIX II

ROOTS FOR BUILDING RHYMING WORDS

From one phonogram or root children can build many words. This is a helpful exercise, since it (1) calls attention to similarities in word forms and in initial consonants, blends, or digraphs, and (2) helps children acquire a better sense of auditory discrimination and identification of sounds.

The teacher may write a few phonograms a day on the chalkboard so children can gain practice in building words. The vowel sound should be discussed and the generalization, such as silent *e*, applied whenever possible.

ab: crab, tab, cab, rabbit, tablet, habit

ace: face, race, place, lace, Grace, brace

ack: quack, back, black, lack, crack, track, tack, pack, clack, sack, shack, stack, snack, smack

ad: bad, Dad, glad, had, lad, sad, mad, pad

ade: made, shade, trade, blade, fade, spade, wade, lemonade

ag: bag, flag, rag, wag, drag, brag, tag, snag, zigzag

age: cage, page, stage, sage, rage

aid: laid, paid, afraid, maid, braid

ail: mail, nail, pail, rail, tail, trail, hail, jail, snail

ain: rain, train, chain, main, plain, brain, grain, drain

air: chair, fair, pair, hair, stair

ake: cake, take, lake, make, shake, rake, wake, sake, bake, brake

alk: talk, walk, chalk, stalk, balk

all: ball, call, fall, hall, tall, wall, small

am: Sam, ham, jam, lamb, hamster, camel, family, ramble

ame: came, game, name, flame, same, tame, frame, shame, lame

amp: camp, lamp, stamp, tramp, clamp, cramp, damp, ramp

an: can, man, pan, ran, than, Nan, began, bran, clan, Dan

ance: chance, dance, glance, prance, France

anch: ranch, branch, Blanche

and: band, land, sand, stand, hand, grand, brand

ane: plane, Jane, cane, mane, pane, vane, crane

ang: bang, hang, sang, rang, sprang, gang, fang, slang

ange: change, strange, range

ank: bank, clank, drank, thank, crank, plank, prank, shrank

ant: plant, grant, pant, slant, chant

ap: cap, map, nap, snap, slap, tap, trap, flap, lap, rap, scrap

ape: scrape, shape, tape, grape, escape, drape, cape

ar: car, far, jar, tar, star, guitar, cigar, scar, bar, bargain, dark

ard: card, yard, hard, lard

are: dare, care, scare, bare, fare, glare, mare, rare, share, square

arge: large, barge, charge

ark: bark, dark, lark, park, shark, spark, mark, hark, Clark

arm: farm, harm, arms, alarm, charm, harmful

arn: barn, yarn, darn

art: smart, apart, part, start, tart, chart, dart, cart

ase: chase, vase, case, base, erase

ash: cash, crash, smash, flash, splash, trash, gash, lash, sash, mash, dash

ast: fast, past, last, mast, blast

aste: paste, waste, taste, baste, haste

at: fat, flat, hat, cat, that, pat, sat, rat, chat, bat, mat, scat, battle

atch: catch, hatch, snatch, patch, match, latch, batch

ate: Kate, state, gate, hate, skate, plate, late, slate, date, mate

ave: save, gave, wave, brave, cave, crave, shave, slave

aw: saw, straw, caw, bawl, jaw, law, paw, raw

ay: day, gay, hay, lay, may, pay, say, tay, way, play, gray, Kay, Fay, jay, Ray, tray, bray, spray, pray, sway, clay, birthday, today

aze: blaze, gaze, graze, glaze
each: teach, reach, beach, preach, bleach, peach, teacher
ead: bead, lead, read, knead
eak: leak, speak, squeak, weak, beak, peak, sneak, streak, creak
eal: meal, real, seal, steal, heal, squeal, veal, deal, peal
eam: cream, team, steam, stream, beam, dream
ean: Jean, mean, lean, beanbag, meaning
eap: leap, cheap, heap, reap
ear: dear, year, tears, ears, hear, near, gear, shear, appear, rear
east: least, yeast, beast, feast
eat: beat, treat, meat, wheat, seat, cheat, neat, bleat, heat
eck: neck, peck, wreck, check, deck, checkers, necklace
ed: bed, fed, led, red, shed, sled, Fred, wedding, Ned, peddle
ee: tree, see, three, free, wee, bee
eed: feed, indeed, need, seed, breed, steed, speed, deed, weed
eel: feel, heel, wheel, steel, wheelbarrow, pinwheel, feelings
een: seen, green, queen, screen, fifteen, between
eep: asleep, deep, keep, sheep, sleep, steep, peep, creep, sweep
eet: meet, feet, sweet, tweet, street, sheet, sleet, beet
eg: leg, keg, beg, beggar, peg
ell: bell, fell, tell, well, shell, sell, smell, yell, Nell
elp: help, yelp
elt: belt, felt, pelt, melt
em: stem, them, gem, hem
end: lend, spend, send, blend, mend, bend
ent: bent, sent, tent, cent, went, dent, lent, spent, rent
ep: step, pep
ess: Bess, less, dress, guess, Jess, recess, chess, bless, confess
est: best, nest, rest, pest, chest, west, vest, test
et: get, let, met, pet, set, yet, jet, net, wet, alphabet, cadet
ew (u):   mew, few, hew, pew, view
ew (oo):   brew, flew, grew, threw, stew, dew, crew, chew, blew
ib: crib, bib, rib, nibble
ice: mice, nice, spice, twice, rice, slice, price
ick: brick, chick, Dick, kick, sick, pick, Nick, quick, stick, thick, trick,
    click, lick, tick, pickle, tickle, wick
id: hid, rid, kid, lid, bid, skid
ide: hide, wide, slide, side, ride, tide, bride, pride
ief: chief, brief, thief
ield: field, shield, yield
ife: wife, life, knife
iff: cliff, sniff, stiff, whiff
ift: gift, lift, swift, shift, drift
ig: big, pig, dig, fig, twig, wig, jig
ight: sight, tight, light, night, right, flight, bright, fight, fright
ike: like, Mike, strike, spike, hike, dike, bike
ild: child, wild, mild
ilk: milk, silk

ill: bill, fill, hill, Jill, kill, mill, still, will, quill, chill, drill, grill, pill, shrill, skill, spill, trill

im: Tim, him, swim, limb, dim, brim, slim, trim, Jim, skim

in: skin, thin, tin, twin, inn, win, chin, fin, pin, shin, violin

ind: behind, kind, mind, wind, hind, blind, rind, bind

ine: mine, nine, vine, valentine, shine, fine, pine, spine, swine

ing: bring, king, ring, sing, spring, sting, swing, string, thing

ink: think, tinkle, drink, pink, sink, wink, clink, mink, link

ip: chip, clip, ship, skip, rip, trip, dip, drip, flip, grip, lip, hip, nip, sip, slip, snip, strip, whip, zip

ipe: ripe, stripe, swipe, wipe, pipe

ire: fire, tire, wire, hire

ise: wise, surprise, rise

iss: miss, kiss, hiss

it: bit, hit, quit, sit, kit, pit, slit, split, wit, flit, knit

itch: witch, hitch, ditch, pitch

ite: bite, kite, white, quite, write, spite, invite, polite, satellite

ive: five, live, alive, dive, hive

ix: six, fix, mix

ize: prize, size

oad: toad, road, load

oak: cloak, soak, croak

oan: Joan, grown, loan, moan, roan

oat: boat, bloat, coat, goat, throat

ob: Bob, job, knob, mob, sob, throb

ock: block, clock, flock, lock, rock, tick-tock, dock, knock, sock, stock, shock, frock, mock, hollyhock, padlock

og: hog, frog, dog, log, fog

oil: boil, spoil, foil, toil, coil

oke: smoke, woke, joke, spoke, yoke, poke, choke

old: cold, gold, hold, scold, sold, told, fold, bold

ole: hole, pole, whole, stole, tadpole, sole, mole

oll: troll, droll, knoll, roll, toll

om: from, Tom, Tom-tom, bomb

one: alone, bone, stone, Jones, telephone, zone, throne, cone

ong: along, ding-dong, long, song, wrong, belong, strong

ood (long oo):   food, mood, brood

ood (short oo):   good, hood, stood, wood

oof: roof, hoof, woof

ook: look, book, took, brook, hook, shook

ool: cool, stool, pool, tool, fool

oom: broom, room, zoom, boom, bloom

oon: balloon, moon, soon, spoon, raccoon, cartoon, cocoon

oop: stoop, coop, hoop, snoop, troop, loop

oot: boot, root, toot, shoot, snoot, hoot

op: crop, top, drop, pop, clop, shop, stop, popcorn, chop, copper, flop, mop, lollipop

ope: rope, hope, telescope, slope, envelope

ore: store, before, bore, chore, explore, score, shore, snore

ork: fork, New York, stork, cork

orn: corn, horn, born, morning, thorn

ose: rose, close, chose, hose, nose, those, suppose, pose

oss: cross, across, boss, moss, Ross, loss, gloss

ost: post, ghost, most, host

ot: dot, got, hot, lot, not, pot, shot, trot, clot, cot, forgot

oud: cloud, loud, proud

ought: thought, brought, bought

ould: should, would, could

our: flour, hour, sour

out: about, shout, stout, pout, snout, trout, without, scout

ow (o): slow, snow, grow, show, throw, blow, crow, bow

ow (ou): cow, how, owl, plow, bowwow

own: brown, clown, crown, drown, gown, town

ox: fox, box

oy: boy, joy, toy, Roy, oyster, enjoy

ub: cub, scrub, rub, grub, tub, shrub, stub, submarine

uch: such, much

uck: duck, truck, cluck, struck, stuck, chuck, luck, buck

ud: mud, Judd, thud, bud

ue: Sue, glue, true, blue

uff: puff, muff, bluff, stuff, snuff, cuff, scuff

ug: bug, rug, dug, hug, mug, plug, pug, shrug, snug, tug

ull (u): dull, gull, hull, skull

ull (short oo): pull, bull, full

um: drum, sum, thumb, chum, crumb, gum, hum, mum, numb

ump: bump, jump, lump, thump, plump, pump, stump, hump

un: fun, sun, run, gun, nun, spun, bun

unch: bunch, lunch, munch, punch, scrunch, crunch

ung: hung, sprung, clung, lung, flung, strung, swung, sung

unk: trunk, skunk, sunk, spunk, hunk, drunk, chunk, shrunk

unt: hunt, stunt, runt, grunt, blunt

up: cup, puppy, supper

urn: burnt, turn, churn

ush: brush, mush, blush, rush, crush, hush

ust: dust, trust, just, crust, thrust, rust, bust

ut: but, cut, hut, nut, shut, strut, butter, buttons

APPENDIX III

PRINCIPLES OF PHONICS

The rich heritage of the English language does not permit a complete analysis of its phonic structure in the few pages of this appendix. Admittedly, this listing of guides for pronunciation is incomplete. The teacher or parent, though, who is seeking guidelines to govern the use of phonics as a reading tool will find that most words in the vocabularies of reading textbooks can be decoded using the principles contained in these pages.

PRONUNCIATION OF CONSONANTS

Consonants in Isolation

1. A consonant sound that changes direction or stops during the course of its production cannot be pronounced in isolation without altering its quality or adding a vowel sound. The following sounds are governed by this rule: *b, d, g, j, k, p, t, w, y, ch, wh.*

2. A consonant sound that is a continuant, that is, one that can be prolonged as long as there is breath supply, can be pronounced in isolation without altering .its quality or adding a vowel sound. The following sounds are governed by this rule: *f, h, l, m, n, r, s, v, z, th* (voiceless), *th* (voiced), *sh, zh, ng.*

Consonant Letters of the Alphabet

B-b:

1. The letter *b* usually has the sound of "b."
2. *mb* combination—*b* is silent when it follows *m* in the same syllable, e.g., *lamb.*
3. *bt* combination—*b* is silent when it is followed by *t* in the same syllable, e.g., *debt.*

C-c:

1. The letter *c* has the sound of "s" when it is followed by the letters *e, i,* or *y,* e.g., *cent, city, cycle, fence, fancy.*
2. The letter *c* usually has the sound of "k" when it is at the end of a word or when it is followed by the letters *a, o, u,* or a consonant, e.g., *antic, cat, coat, cup, clean.*
3. *ch* combination—See digraph *ch.*
4. *ci* combination
   a. In initial position, this combination is pronounced according to number 1 above.
   b. In medial position, this combination usually has the sound of "sh" when followed by an unstressed vowel, e.g., *social.*
5. *ck* combination—*c* is silent when followed by the letter *k* in the same syllable.
6. *sc* combination
   a. In initial position, the letter *c* often is silent in this combination and the letter *s* has its own sound. Exceptions are *score, scare.*
   b. In medial position, this combination usually has the sound of "sh" when followed by an unstressed vowel, e.g., *conscious.*

D-d:

1. The letter *d* usually has the sound of "d."
2. *dg* combination—This combination always is pronounced as "j" (soft *g*), e.g., *badge,* except when *d* and *g* are separate syllables, e.g., *headgear.*
3. *dj* combination—This combination usually is pronounced as "j" (soft *g*), e.g., *adjust.*
4. *ed* endings
   a. If the stem of the verb ends in *t* or *d,* the suffix *ed* usually is pronounced as a separate syllable, e.g., *wanted, loaded.*
   b. If the stem of the verb ends in a vowel or a voiced consonant other than *d,* the suffix *ed* has the sound of "d," e.g., *dittoed, dried, called, hugged.*
   c. If the stem of the verb ends in a voiceless consonant other than *t,* the suffix *ed* has the sound of "t," e.g., *laughed, walked.*

F-f:

1. The letter *f* is never silent in a word and has the sound of "f," e.g., *fun, puff.* An exception is the word *of,* in which the letter has the sound of "v."

G-g:

1. Initial *g,* followed by *a, o, u,* or a consonant letter, usually has the sound of "g" (hard *g*), e.g., *gate, go, gum, green, ghost.*
2. Medial *g,* followed by *a, o, u,* or a consonant letter, usually has the sound of "g" (hard *g*) except when the *gh* combination is found, e.g., *began, ago, ague, hungry.*
3. Initial *g,* followed by *i* or *e,* may have the sound of "g" (hard *g*) or "j" (soft *g*), e.g., *give, get* (hard *g*); *gin, gentle* (soft *g*).
4. Medial *g,* followed by *i* or *e,* usually is pronounced as "j" (soft *g*), e.g., *digest, register.*
5. Initial *g,* followed by *y,* usually has the sound of "j" (soft *g*), e.g., *gypsy.*
6. Final *g,* when not a part of the digraph *ng,* has the sound of "g" (hard *g*), e.g., *pig.*
7. Final *ge* usually has the sound of "j" (soft *g*), e.g., *age,* although many such words still retain an approximation of their original French pronunciation, e.g., *beige* ("bazh"), *rouge* ("roozh").
8. *dg* combination—See consonant *d,* number 2.
9. *gh* combination—See digraph *gh.*
10. *gm* and *gn* combinations—The letter *g* is silent before *m* or *n* in the same syllable, e.g., *phlegm, gnaw.*
11. *ng* combination—See digraph *ng.*

H-h:

1. Initial *h* in a word or syllable usually has the sound of "h," e.g., *hand,* although it is silent in certain words, e.g., *hour, heir, honor, honest,* and their derivatives.
2. *ch* combination—See digraph *ch.*
3. *gh* combination—See digraph *gh.*
4. *kh* combination—The letter *h* usually is silent when it follows *k* in the same syllable, e.g., *khaki.*
5. *ph* combination—See digraph *ph.*
6. *rh* combination—The letter *h* usually is silent when it follows *r* in the same syllable, e.g., *rhyme.*
7. *th* combination—See digraph *th.*
8. *wh* combination—See digraph *wh.*

J-j:

1. The letter *j* usually has the sound of "j" (soft *g*), e.g., *jump, major.*
2. *dj* combination—See consonant *d,* number 3.

K-k:

1. The letter *k* usually has the sound of "k," e.g., *keep, basket, cook.*
2. *ck* combination—See consonant *c*, number 5.
3. *kh* combination—See consonant *h*, number 4.
4. *kn* combination—The letter *k* is silent before *n* in the same syllable, e.g., *know.*

L-l:

1. The letter *l* usually has the sound of "l," e.g., *let, pillow, bell,* although there are numerous words in which *l* is silent (see below).
2. *ld* combination—Both letters usually are sounded as a blend, e.g., *field,* except in *could, would, should,* and their derivatives, when *l* is silent.
3. *lf* combination
   a. The letter *l* usually is silent when this combination follows the letter *a* in the same syllable, e.g., *half.*
   b. Both letters usually are sounded as a blend when this combination follows the letters *e, o,* or *u* in the same syllable, e.g., *elf, golf, gulf.*
4. *lk* combination
   a. The letter *l* usually is silent when this combination follows the letters *a* or *o* in the same syllable, e.g., *walk, yolk.*
   b. Both letters are sounded as a blend when this combination follows the letters *e, i,* or *u* in the same syllable, e.g., *elk, milk, bulk.*
5. *lm* combination
   a. The letter *l* is usually silent when this combination follows the letters *a* or *o* in the same syllable, e.g., *calm, holm.*
   b. Both letters are sounded as a blend when this combination follows the letters *e* ("ea") or *i,* e.g., *elm, film.*
6. *ln* combination—The letter *l* usually is silent when followed by *n* in the same syllable, e.g., *Lincoln.*
7. *lv* combination
   a. The letter *l* usually is silent when this combination follows the letter *a* in the same syllable, e.g., *halve.*
   b. Both letters are sounded as a blend when this combination follows the letters *e* or *o* in the same syllable, e.g., *delve, solve.*

M-m:

1. The letter *m* usually has the sound of "m," e.g., *man, camera, ham.*
2. *gm* combination—See consonant *g*, number 10.
3. *lm* combination—See consonant *l*, number 5.
4. *mb* combination—See consonant *b*, number 2.
5. *mn* combination
   a. When this combination is in the initial position, the letter *m* is silent, e.g., *mnemonic.*
   b. When this combination is in the final position, the letter *n* is silent, e.g., *hymn.*

N-n:

1. The letter *n* usually has the sound of "n," e.g., *nine, pony.*
2. When the letter *n* is followed by *k, g,* or *x,* it usually has the sound of *ng,* e.g., *thank, singer, anxious.* However, if a word or syllable ends in *nge,* the *n* usually retains the sound of "n," e.g., *orange.*
3. *gn* combination—See consonant *g,* number 10.
4. *kn* combination—See consonant *k,* number 4.
5. *mn* combination—See consonant *m,* number 5.
6. *ng* combination—See digraph *ng.*
7. *pn* combination—The letter *p* usually is silent before *n* in the same syllable, e.g., *pneumonia.*

P-p:

1. The letter *p* usually has the sound of "p," e.g., *popcorn, hop.*
2. *pn* combination—See consonant *n,* number 7.
3. *ps* combination—When this combination is in the initial position, the letter *p* is silent, e.g., *psalm.*
4. *pt* combination—When this combination is in initial position, the letter *p* is silent, e.g., *ptarmigan.*

Q-q:

1. The letter *q* is always followed by the letter *u.* This combination usually has the sound of "kw," e.g., *queen,* although in the medial or final position it may have the sound of "k," e.g., *conquer, liquor, antique.*

R-r:

1. All Americans pronounce initial *r,* as in *red,* the same. Most Americans give a modified pronunciation of *r* in medial and final positions.
2. *rh* combination—See letter *h,* number 6.
3. Vowel-*r* combination—The vowel letter has its sound modified or controlled by the *r,* e.g., *car, learn, fern, bird, word, for, fur.*
4. *wr* combination—The letter *w* is silent when it precedes *r* in the same syllable, e.g., *write.*

S-s:

1. Initial *s* always has the sound of "s," e.g., *sun.*
2. Medial *s* may have the sound of "s," e.g., *mist,* or "z," e.g., *used.*
3. Final *s* has the sound of "s"
   a. When it follows a voiceless consonant to form the plural of a noun, e.g., *cats.*
   b. When it is doubled, e.g., *miss.*
   c. When it follows a voiceless consonant to form the third-person singular of a verb, e.g., *takes.*

    d. When it follows *a, i, o, u,* or *y* (except as noted in number 4), e.g., *gas, this, chaos, us.*

4. Final *s* has the sound of "z"
   a. When it follows a voiced consonant to form the plural of a noun, e.g., *dogs.*
   b. When it follows a vowel or a voiced consonant to form the third-person singular of a verb, e.g., *rubs, plays, has.*

5. *s* has the sound of "sh" in *sugar, sure,* and their derivatives

6. *s* is silent in a few words, e.g., *isle, island.*

7. *lse, nse, pse, rse* combinations—In these word endings, the *s* usually has the sound of "s,", e.g., *pulse, tense, corpse, purse.*

8. *ps* combination—See consonant *p*, number 3.

9. *sci* combination—See consonant *c*, number 6.

10. *se* combination—When this combination is final and follows a vowel, *s* may have either the sound of "s" or "z," e.g., *chase, choose.*

11. *sh* combination—See digraph *sh*.

12. *si* combination
    a. This combination usually has the "sh" sound
       (1) When it is followed by an unstressed vowel or syllable consonant, e.g., *pension.*
       (2) When it follows a syllable that ends in an *s*, e.g., *discussion.*
       (3) When the root word has an *s* where the derived word begins, e.g., *tense–tension.*
    (b) This combination usually has the "zh" sound
       (1) When it follows a syllable that does not end in *s*, e.g., *division.*
       (2) When the root word does not have an *s* where the derived word begins, e.g., *explode–explosion.*

13. *ss* combination—Medial *ss* usually has the sound of "s" in words derived from others ending in *ss*, e.g., *classify.*

T-t:

1. The letter *t* usually has the sound of "t," e.g., *tent, kitten,* although in words ending in *stle* and *sten* it is silent, e.g., *castle, listen.* It is silent also in such words as *Christmas* and *often.*

2. *th* combination—See digraph *th*.

3. *tial, tient,* and *tious* combinations—The *ti* usually has the sound of "sh," e.g., *partial, patient, cautious,* when it is followed by an unstressed vowel or syllabic consonant.

4. *tion* combination—The *ti* usually has the sound of "sh," e.g., *nation,* as indicated in number 3, although it may be pronounced as "ch," e.g., *question.*

5. *ture* combination—The *tu* usually has the sound of "ch," e.g., *nature.*

V-v:

1. The letter *v* usually has the sound of "v," e.g., *valentine, seven, five.*

W-w:

1. Initial or medial *w* usually has the sound of "w," e.g., *wagon, sandwich*.
2. Final *w* may be silent, e.g., *yellow*, or may participate as a part of the vowel sound, e.g., *blew, raw, cow*.
3. Initial or medial *w* sometimes is silent before the sounds of short *oo* and long *oo*, e.g., *two, who*, and their derivatives.
4. Medial *w* sometimes is silent before an unaccented syllable, e.g., *answer*.

X-x:

1. Initial *x* usually has the sound of "z," e.g., *xylophone*.
2. Medial or final *x* usually has the sound of "ks," e.g., *saxophone, box*.
3. *ex* combination—In this combination, the letter *x* usually has the sound of "gz" when followed by a stressed or semistressed vowel, e.g., *example, exhibit* (silent *h*); otherwise it has the sound of "ks," e.g., *exercise*.

Y-y:

1. In initial position in a word or syllable, the letter *y* has the sound of "y," e.g., *you, barnyard*.
2. In other positions, *y* usually functions as a vowel and is pronounced as long *i* or short *i*. See vowel rules.

Z-z:

1. The letter *z* usually has the sound of "z," e.g., *zoo, lazy, buzz*.

Consonant Digraphs

Ch-ch:

1. *ch* usually has the sound of "ch," e.g., *chair, kitchen, much*, although it may have the sound of "k" in words of Greek origin, e.g., *Christmas, character*, or the sound of "sh" in words of French origin, e.g., *chamois, machine*.
2. *chr* combination—Initial *chr* usually has the sound of "kr," e.g., *Christmas, chrome*.
3. *sch* combination—Initial *sch* has the sound of "sk" in common English words, e.g., *school, scholar*. Exceptions are proper names and words of Germanic origin.

Gh-gh:

1. Initial *gh* always has the sound of "g" (hard *g*), e.g., *ghost*.
2. *augh(t)* combination
   a. *gh* is silent when *au* has the sound of "aw," e.g., *caught, daughter*.
   b. *gh* has the sound of "f" when *au* has the sound usually heard in such words as *laugh* and *draught*. This *au* sound has a regional variation from the short *a* to sounds indicated by diacritical marking as "ă" and "ä."

3. *eigh(t)* combination—*gh* is silent, but *ei* may have the sound of long *a*, e.g., *eight*, *neighbor*, or long *i*, e.g., *height*.
4. *igh(t)* combination—*gh* is silent and *i* has the sound of long *i*, e.g., *sigh*, *light*.
5. *ough* combination
   a. *gh* is silent when *ou* has the sound of long *o*, e.g., *dough*, *though*.
   b. *gh* is silent when *ou* has the sound of the diphthong *ow*, e.g., *bough*, *plough*.
   c. *gh* is silent when *ou* has the sound of long *oo*, e.g., *through*, *slough*.
   d. *gh* has the sound of "f" when *ou* has the short *u* sound, *enough*, *tough*.
   e. *gh* has the sound of "f" when *ou* has the sound of "aw," e.g., *cough*.
6. *ought* combination—*gh* is silent and *ou* usually has the sound of "aw," e.g., *bought*.

Ng:

1. Medial *ng*, in words formed from verbs by the addition of the suffixes *er* and *ing*, has the sound of "ng" alone, e.g., *singer*, *bringing*.
2. Medial *ng* has the sound of "ng" plus "g" (hard g)
   a. In words formed from adjectives by the addition of the suffixes *er* and *est*, e.g., *longer*, *longest*.
   b. In words other than those derived from verbs and adjectives, e.g., *jungle*, *finger*.
3. Final *ng* has the sound of "ng" alone, e.g., *ring*.
4. *nge* combination—This combination at the end of a word ordinarily has the sound of "n" plus "j" (soft g) and retains this pronunciation in derived words, e.g., *strange–stranger–strangest*.

Ph-ph:

1. *ph* usually has the sound of "f" when the combination appears within the same syllable, e.g., *phonograph*, *elephant*, *Philip* (but note the "v" sound in *Stephen*).
2. When *p* and *h* occur in successive syllables, *p* has the sound of "p," e.g., *shepherd*.

Sh-sh:

1. *sh* always has the sound of "sh," e.g., *shoe*, *washing*, *fish*, unless the two letters appear in separate syllables, e.g., *crosshatch*.

Th-th:

1. Initial *th* sound of *th* voiceless (*thumb*) in nouns, verbs, adjectives, and those adverbs derived from adjectives, e.g., *thimble*, *thank*, *thick*, *thinly*.
2. Initial *th* has the sound of the *th* voiced (*they*) in pronouns, conjunctions, and those adverbs and their derivatives not derived from adjectives, e.g., *them*, *than*, *then*, *themselves*.
3. Final *th* usually has the sound of *th* voiceless, e.g., *south*.

4. *the* combination—When this combination is used as a word ending, *th* usually is voiced and the *e* is silent, e.g., *bathe*.
5. *ths* combination—When this combination is used as a word ending
   a. *th* usually is voiceless (1) if it is preceded by a short vowel, e.g., *breaths*; (2) if it is preceded by a consonant, including *r*, e.g., *months*, *births*.
   b. *th* usually is voiced after a diphthong, e.g., *booths*, *mouths*.

Wh-wh:

1. *wh* usually has the sound of "hw," e.g., *what, anywhere*, except when followed by the letter *o*. In the latter case, the *w* usually is silent and the digraph has the sound of "h," e.g., *who, whole*.
2. There is a definite tendency to pronounce *wh* as "w" in many common English words, e.g., *what, where, when, why*, etc.

PRONUNCIATION OF VOWELS

Short-Vowel Rule

1. An initial or medial vowel in a word or syllable usually has the short sound when it is the only vowel in a word, e.g., *at, pet, pig, doll, nut, hymn*.

Long-Vowel Rules

1. A final vowel (*a, e, o, u*) usually has its long sound when it is the only vowel in a word, e.g., *me, go*, or in a syllable, e.g., *open, taken*.
2. A final *i* or *y* in a word or syllable may either have the long *i* sound, e.g., *final, my*, or have the short *i* sound, e.g., *division, city*.
3. When two vowels appear together in a word or syllable, the first vowel usually is long and the second vowel silent, e.g., *eat, tree, cue, boat, toe, rain, say, pie*.
4. When two vowels appear in a word or syllable and one of them is final *e*, the first vowel usually is long and the final *e* silent, e.g., *rake, eve, kite, home, mule, rhyme*.

Followed by *w* or *l*

1. If *a* is the only vowel in a word or syllable and is followed by *w* or *l*, it has neither the long nor the short sound, but usually has the sound of "aw," e.g., *law, ball*.

Double *o*

1. If two *os* appear together in a word or a syllable, they have the sound of short *oo* as in *book* or long *oo* as in *moon*.

Vowels Followed by *r*

A single vowel followed by *r* in a word or syllable has neither its long nor its short sound, but is modified and controlled by the consonant *r:*

1. *e, i, u* and *y* followed by *r* usually are combined with *r* and pronounced as "er," e.g., *her, bird, fur, myrtle.*
2. *a* followed by *r* usually has the sound of "ah," e.g., *arm, car.*
3. *o* followed by *r* usually has the sound of "aw," e.g., *corn;* when *o* is followed by *r* and preceded by *w*, the combination *or* may have the sound of "er," e.g., *work.*

INDEX

A "T" following a page number indicates that a table appears on that page.